Collector's Guide to

with Values

by
Fred Diehl

Text and photographs by the author

Published by   **Hobby House Press**
Grantsville, Maryland 21536
www.hobbyhouse.com

Dedication

I would like to dedicate this book to various members of my family.
To my late father who was always a catalyst for my collecting hobbies,
to my mother, Esther who continues to be there to support me to this day,
and to my son, Andy, whom I hope will become a consummate collector like his father.

Additional copies of this book may be purchased at $19.95 (plus postage and handling) from
Hobby House Press, Inc.
1 Corporate Drive, Grantsville, MD 21536
1-800-554-1447
www.hobbyhouse.com
or from your favorite bookstore or dealer.
©2001 Fred Diehl

Printed in the United States of America

ISBN: 0-87588-600-0

Table of Contents

Acknowledgements

The author would like to thank several people who helped in some way with gathering information for this book. These fine individuals are listed here in no specific order or magnitude of gratitude. Thanks to all.

Bonnie Rayborn, my eBay and Internet *My Merry* friend who donated the magic set, helped me with the 1959 catalog copy and provided much information regarding set descriptions.

Karen Caviale, editor of *Barbie® Bazaar* magazine with the *Barbie®* set information in general. *Barbie® Bazaar* magazine, 5711 8th Avenue, Kenosha, WI 53140

Gina Laprie who graciously donated a Teeter Time watch to this cause through a mutual friend, Judy Azzolina, who loaned me a *My Merry* make-up set and never asked for its return.

Laural Schwing, who provided some early information on the *Skipper®* closets before I had them myself.

Carmen Tickal, Marcy Feldt, and Suzanne Bowns for helping me find various *My Merry* deals throughout the years.

Introduction

During the 1950's and 1960's, the Merry Manufacturing Company of Cincinnati, Ohio produced a very fascinating and unique line of children's toys. Originally designed as accessories for doll and dollhouse play, the *My Merry* play sets have become very collectible for not only doll fanciers, but miniaturists as well.

Every *My Merry* set is a fascinating toy in its own right. Each contained accessories that help support a specific theme (kitchen, laundry, party, etc.). In addition, genuine brand-name products of the day were included. Not only were the packages reproduced in true form, but also the contents were real as well. A small bottle of *Windex* actually contained the liquid glass cleaner. A package of *Duz* laundry soap contained the soap powder while a box of *Kleenex* came with the real paper product as well. Many *My Merry* pieces are occasionally found loose in miscellaneous boxes at doll shows. Most serious doll collectors usually have at least one or two pieces somewhere in their collections, many not even knowing that the little accessory is a *My Merry* piece at all.

Finding a complete, mint set involves locating a toy that a child actually restrained from opening and playing with, thereby using the contents. As such, complete sets are harder to find and are desired by serious collectors. The safety standards of today would almost completely prohibit the sale of these sets for child's play due to the included chemicals and small parts. However, they are indeed charming toys and provide a glimpse back to the post World War II era of domestic product expansion in America.

My Merry sets came in many different configurations. *My Merry* "shops" contained items representative of an actual store (i.e. cosmetic, hobby etc.) while the "closet" series had items that could be found in a home organized according to a specific use. The "Diaper Closet" has baby supplies, while the "Hostess Closet" contained party items and so forth. Some boxes may have originally had a cellophane shrink-wrap covering to keep the small pieces intact or a clear plastic cover sheet to secure the box openings. It is a wonder that those not sealed ever stayed complete in the store and through the years. Most boxes were 5" to 10" wide and 1" to 2" deep. Cardboard awnings of shops could be folded out while the closets had a front cover "closet door". The later sets used the term *Miss Merry* frequently and seemed to have more plastic accessories, less cardboard and fewer name-brand products. These items were often packed in plastic trays that slid out of the window box, not unlike holiday candy. Still later sets were blister-carded.

Most accessories are marked "Merry Mfg." or "*My Merry*", but a few are unmarked as well. Many of the same accessories were used in various sets and there were some color and style variations in the plastic items as well as substitute pieces (i.e. the plastic boxed checkers vs. the cardboard punch-out pieces). Early Merry Manufacturing boxes are marked "Cincinnati 3, Ohio" while later boxes (printed with a copyright date after 1959) are marked "Cincinnati 15, Ohio". Since the Merry Manufacturing Company is no longer in business, it seems that the collectors of today will have to take a giant step back in time when life was simpler and write the history of *My Merry*.

About This Book

The volume in your hands is a labor of love. The idea for this book was initially conceived several years ago and was actually going to be a joint venture. *Collector's Guide to My Merry* has become a solo project with the help of some fine *My Merry* collector friends.

The author has personally located over 160 different sets to date with many more known *My Merry* toy items. Each section of this guide describes every set with as much detail and information as is available to date. Included are the copyright and/or catalog date, original price, stock number, set size (width, depth and thickness) and the known contents of each set. Only *My Merry* sets available to the author at the time of printing are included here.

The book is generally laid out according to the era in which a given set was manufactured. The early period includes items from 1950 through 1956. The mid to late 1950's era covers items offered from 1957 through 1959. The *My Merry* logo changed in 1959 and that particular catalog shows sets with both styles of graphics. The next section includes the early 1960s as evidenced in the 1961 catalog. Many complete set series were shown in this catalog and this era seems to be a true favorite among collectors. The early to mid 1960's are covered in the next chapter. Plastic trays and clear boxes were now used extensively in the packaging. The *Barbie*®-related sets were offered in this period and *My Merry* matured and came into its own in this era.

The later 1960's and early 1970's almost exclusively involved the use of blister-carded items and package deals with many set identities themselves (names, numbers) being lost in the mass-packaging efforts. Merry Toys produced in the late 1970's and early 1980's are included in the last era-based chapter.

The Checklist and Price Guide is the final section of this book. It includes the name of the item, year it was produced, the stock number, low and high values, and a place to check off if you own specific items.

The sets shown are the best examples that the author has located to date. With the packages being primarily cardboard, time has indeed taken its toll on many sets. Contents have evaporated, cardboard has become soiled or torn and powder has often escaped its confines and covered the rest of the set. Obviously, there are some sets in better condition residing in collections throughout the country. Sets in this book are generally organized alphabetically within the chapters. Exceptions to this are sets falling within a specific series such as the stores and closets, which are listed numerically. This book is not intended to be a complete showing of sets within a given time period or series. Nor is it meant to present the best example in existence for a given item. The author has tried to provide images of the items in the best and most complete condition as possible. For every set in the book, there probably exists a set somewhere that is 100% complete and mint in a mint package. If you are the proud owner of a set such as this, or one that is slightly different, consider yourself fortunate, as many sets did not survive. Through the years, pieces were also lost and replaced.

Many Merry toys of the later blister-carded and Arco era are not shown in this volume in order to more completely show the earlier sets. Also missing are any catalog reprints, miscellaneous *My Merry* commercial advertisements, shipping cartons, set variations and non-Merry copies of Merry sets. Hopefully, interest in *My Merry* will warrant and generate a second volume! The author photographed all images in the book with a Leica R4 or a Nikon F2 on Kodachrome 200 film. It is for the collectors and lovers of toys themselves that this book was conceived. Enjoy.

Collecting My Merry

With the definitive collecting guide to *My Merry* (actually, the *only* guide to *My Merry*) now in hand, where does a collector start? Obviously, the fact that you opened this book at all shows some interest on your part in these toys. As with a collection of anything, the collector or potential collector needs to make some initial decisions to guide him or her during the actual collecting phase.

What attracts you to *My Merry*? If you are primarily a miniature enthusiast, collecting loose items is probably the best method of building a *My Merry* collection. Many loose items can be found for rather reasonable prices at doll shows as well as miniature and dollhouse events. There is usually a suitable quantity available and a buyer can actually shop for piece condition and price without needing to make unnecessary "impulse" purchases. A collection of *My Merry* items displays quite well in its own right and can be set apart, or included with, other toy collections such as dolls, houses, vehicles, miniatures, etc. *My Merry* can even compliment collections of real-life kitchen and bath product containers of the 50's and 60's. These packages are now being sought after and displayed prominently by the baby boomers who remember mom using *Soilax* cleaner or *Coets* make-up removing pads. The possibilities are endless. Keep in mind that a piece that is severely damaged and does not display well (i.e., does not even have one "good" side) is probably not a good purchase.

If you find the *overall* toy set aspect of *My Merry* charming, the acquisition of boxed sets will probably provide the most satisfaction. Collecting complete sets is, however, a somewhat more difficult endeavor. When in the market and mood to buy *My Merry* sets, decide which ones you really want. Do you wish to obtain one of *every* set produced (as the author did), or just an example or two of each *series*? Do you wish to specialize with just the ones that relate to babies and dolls, or just the stores (the author's favorite),

or the closets (the most diverse)? Having this in mind can be an advantage as you travel amidst the maze of what is available versus your available spending money and display space. Collecting will be far easier now with this book in hand! Happily, collecting *My Merry* is not a hobby for the rich. Quite the opposite; this particular toy is relatively inexpensive to acquire, compared to many of its contemporaries. Even the most expensive sets are still quite reasonable.

At the time of purchase, the two "C's" of *My Merry* collecting, condition and completeness, must be considered. Condition of anything is *very* subjective. Forget about grading scales and precise, named grading classes (i.e. very good, excellent, mint). As you look at a set, the question must be asked, "Is this set nice enough to display among my other items, or will I be discouraged with its condition every time I look at it?" Only the collector can decide this. This subjective question about condition is the only way that you can determine if the set is good enough for you. Try not to buy junk, but do not pass up on an enjoyable hobby holding out for perfection on each item. Upgrading pieces in any collecting arena is part of the process and yes, part of the fun as well.

Some sets may have moderate corner crushes, slight tears and light soiling and/or fading, yet still retain the original charisma of the set and will display nicely, even though a verbal description of said set sounds terrible. Others, which would verbally describe to be in much better shape, may, in reality, neither present nor display well. This is a good reason for trying to acquire a set in person, or insisting upon a reasonable return privilege. Small tears, especially inherent in the sides of the store and closet-series box openings, are quite easily repaired with a small amount of white glue and display quite well after this simple fix. Price should also be factored into condition. For example, the author rejected the purchase of a Toy Closet because it not only had the corner was quite severly water damaged, but the asking price was as much as a near-perfect example should be. If the price is right, buy any set for included parts, though. This leads to set completeness.

Armed with this book, you will hopefully be able to determine if a given set for sale is complete. There are some slight variations in set contents and in reality, there will be some omissions within this volume. This should also be considered when counting a set's contents. A near complete set in nice shape should not be turned down because of a missing piece or two. As stated earlier, loose pieces do indeed turn up. Right now, there are no real elusive *My Merry* pieces, so everything is available to those who have reasonable patience. If a set is nowhere near complete, the condition of the box itself should be the deciding factor. An above average box at the right price is a decent purchase since a complete set in a lesser box may be just around the corner. Again,

as with any collectible item, the buyer should always be aware of his or her available display/storage space as well as capital and should spend accordingly.

A word now about price guides. A value guide is indeed included in the back of this book. Prices for *My Merry* sets can vary quite a bit between sellers and from set to set. The prices in this guide are just that—-*guide* prices. A collector may have to pay more for a very pristine set, while bargains can often be had as well. If a collector desires a particular set, then by all means, emotion should be taken into account and should override the value guide—words of wisdom spoken by a true collector. The author, in his quest for a complete *My Merry* collection, has admittedly overpaid for sets on occasion.

In short, the collector should be armed with information, a general idea as to what is desired and a little bit of spending money to accomplish this goal. Happy collecting!

Early My Merry Sets

(1950-1956)

The period of 1950 through 1959 is generally considered to be the golden age of *My Merry* toys. Plastic pieces were kept to a minimum and the sets of this era contain the most name-brand products. Long before blister carding was the norm, these packages were all cardboard with minimal pilfering protection, indicative of a full-service toy store/hobby shop rather than a self-service store.

The sets of this era are also quite diverse in both packaging and contents. Early boxes were printed in two colors only while full color graphics were standard by 1955. The set themes ranged from the standard *My Merry*

fare of make-up and cleaning goods to shoe shining kits and a set that actually permitted the growing of live radishes!

This book breaks down the 1950's era into two groupings, early and late, to help the collector. Sets from 1950 have script printing with only a vague attempt at a trademark style of writing. The *My Merry* logo of 1952 through 1956 inclusive is black script and generally printed in a style recognizable as a *My Merry* set. Sets with this style of printing are indeed the earliest sets and form the basis for a line of toys that fascinated children for over three decades.

MY DOLLY'S MERRY MAKE-UP
"Just Like Mommy's"

YEAR: **1950**
STOCK NUMBER: **unknown**
PRICE: **unknown**
SIZE: **3-1/2in (8.9cm)W x 3-1/2in (9cm)H x 7/8 in (2.2cm)T**
KNOWN CONTENTS:
* glass bottle of *Merry Cherry*, presumably perfume
* gold colored tube of lipstick
* pink cardboard box of play make-up

Notes:
This is the earliest set the author has encountered. The package colors are unique on this set as only two are printed- blue and pink. The set has a totally different and a slightly plainer appearance than later sets. The back of the box reads:

> **COPYRIGHT 1950**
> **EUGENE L. ACH**
> **437 E. 5th St.711 SYCAMORE STREET**
> **CINCINNATI 2, O.**

There is no reference at all to the Merry Manufacturing Company anywhere on this piece! Eugene L. Ach was the owner of what developed into the Merry Manufacturing Co. This may explain why he is listed so prominently on the package.

WASH-N-WAVE SET

YEAR: **1950**
STOCK NUMBER: **unknown**
PRICE: **unknown**
SIZE: **4-1/2in (11.4 cm) x 4 3/8in (11.1cm) x 1in (2.5cm)**

KNOWN CONTENTS:
- plastic comb
- washcloth
- 2 glass bottles of *Merry* Wave set
- 6 pink plastic hair curlers

Notes:

This is the second earliest set the author has encountered. The package colors are again almost unique on this set as only two are printed—blue and pink. Two variations exist. One has a primarily blue top and the other primarily white. The set also has a somewhat plain appearance. This set contains the first reference to the Merry Manufacturing Company! The back of the box reads:

**COPYRIGHT 1950
MERRY MANUFACTURING CO.,
EUGENE L. ACH
711 SYCAMORE STREET
CINCINNATI 2, OHIO**

YEAR: **1952**
STOCK NUMBER: **unknown**
PRICE: **unknown**
SIZE: **7in (17.8cm) x 7in (17.8cm) x
7/8in (2.2cm)**

KNOWN CONTENTS:
- white wooden cuticle pencil
- emery board
- glass bottle of *My Merry* nail polish
- wooden cuticle tool
- six pink plastic hair rollers
- glass bottle of *My Merry* perfume
- brown cardboard tube of lipstick
- pink cardboard can of talc
- pink terry cloth towel
- bottle of nail polish remover
- glass bottle of *My Merry* wave set
- glass bottle of *My Merry* shampoo

Notes:
This very early set has the text "SAFE AND HARMLESS" inside with the ingredients of the products stated, i.e. "perfume is non-alcoholic, lipstick is pomade", etc. This printing is on the inside back vertical edge of the package.

SONNY'S SHAVE 'N SHINE SET

YEAR: 1952
STOCK NUMBER: unknown
PRICE: unknown
**SIZE: 7in (17.8cm) x 7in (17.8cm) x
       7/8in (2.2cm)**

KNOWN CONTENTS:
- wooden-handled shoe polish applicator
- shoe polish cloth
- can of *Shinola* shoe polish
- cardboard box of *GEM* razor blades
  (set box marked "HARMLESS PAPER
  BLADES")
- red wooden shaving brush
- plastic safety razor
- wooden soap dish with crown-embossed
  bar of soap
- yellow wooden-handled clothes brush

Notes:
This early set has no text stating "SAFE AND
HARMLESS" as the Beauty set has, although
of the same vintage.

DOLLY'S FACIAL KIT
"Actually Cleans Vinyl, Latex and Plastic Dolls"

YEAR: 1953
STOCK NUMBER: **unknown**
PRICE: **unknown**
SIZE: **8-1/2in (21.3cm) x 4-1/2in (11.2cm) x 7/8in (23.2cm)**

<u>**KNOWN CONTENTS:**</u>

- white tube of *My Merry* hand lotion
- box of *My Merry* "COTTON TAIL" cotton
- pink plastic make-up cape
- yellow powder puff w/small attached flower
- pink cardboard can of talc
- glass bottle of *My Merry* "Dolly Cleanser"
- 3 wooden cotton swabs
- blue/white cardboard box of *Scotties* tissues

Notes:
Another one of the early 1950's sets with the unique period graphics on the box lid. A clear plastic band wrapped horizontally around the box underneath the lid held the contents in place.

GROW-A-GARDEN
"in 3 days"

YEAR: 1953
STOCK NUMBER: unknown
PRICE: unknown
SIZE: 12in (30.5cm) x 3-1/2in (8.9cm) x 1-3/4in (4.4cm)
KNOWN CONTENTS:
- cardboard box of *My Merry* radish seeds
- large clear plastic box with lid
- sealed plastic bag of "magic soil"
- yellow plastic watering can
- pink plastic shovel

Notes:
Without a doubt, the most unusual *My Merry* set encountered by the author in eight years of collecting. This is the only set that adds play value via the actual growing of agriculture products! One has to wonder about the choice of radishes as the given plant to grow. Either most of the sets produced were in fact played with or they were thrown out with other garden products. In any case, very few survived and this is truly a unique addition to a *My Merry* collection and one of the author's favorites.

SHAVING SET
"Just Like Dad's"

YEAR: **1953**
STOCK NUMBER: **unknown**
PRICE: **unknown**
SIZE: **4-1/2in (11.2cm) x 4-1/2in (11.2cm) x 7/8in (2.2cm)**

KNOWN CONTENTS:
- cardboard box of *PAL* razor blades
- red wooden shaving brush with white bristles
- wooden soap dish with embossed bar of soap
- red plastic razor

Notes:
None

SHOE SHINING SET
"Just Like Dad's"

YEAR: **1953**
STOCK NUMBER: **unknown**
PRICE: **unknown**
SIZE: **4-1/2in (11.4cm) x 4-1/2in (11.4cm) x 1in (2.5cm)**

KNOWN CONTENTS:
- shoe shining cloth
- metal tin of *Shinola* brand shoe polish
- red-handled polish applicator

Notes:
While small, this set appeals to *Shinola* collectors as well as *My Merry* fanciers. For its size, this is one of the most valuable sets

"Look! Curly hair just like Mommy's and Dolly's too"

YEAR: **1953**
STOCK NUMBER: **unknown**
PRICE: **unknown**
SIZE: **4-1/2in (11.2cm) x 4-1/2in (11.2cm) x 7/8in (2.2cm)**

KNOWN CONTENTS:
- blue terry washcloth
- glass bottle of *My Merry* shampoo
- 6 pink plastic curlers
- glass bottle of *My Merry* wave set

Notes:
None

DOLL'YS BATH SET

YEAR: **1955**
STOCK NUMBER: **unknown**
PRICE: **unknown**
SIZE: **7-1/4in (18.4cm) x 5-1/2in (14cm) x 1-1/4in (3.2cm)**

KNOWN CONTENTS:

* plastic tube of *My Merry* "Pssst" toy deodorant
* blue terry cloth towel
* glass bottle of *My Merry* "Cologne #5"
* red cardboard canister of *My Merry* bath salts #1
* silver cardboard canister of *My Merry* talc
* green cardboard canister of *My Merry* foot powder
* gold cardboard canister of *My Merry* bath salts #2
* glass bottle of *My Merry* shampoo
* pink *Dupont* cellulose sponge with paper label
* pink terry cloth washcloth **or**
* bar of *Ivory* soap

Notes:
With all of the bottles and canisters, this is one of the more interesting of the early sets.

FINGER AND TOE MANICURE
"With Pretend Stick-on Nails"

YEAR: **1955**
STOCK NUMBER: **unknown**
PRICE: **unknown**
SIZE: **8in (20.3cm) x 4-1/2in (11.4cm)
        x 3/4in (1.9m)**

KNOWN CONTENTS:

*   metal nail file
*   emery board
*   red plastic finger rest
*   dark blue cardboard peel-off sheets containing play "nails"
*   wooden cuticle tool
*   red wooden colored cuticle pencil containing white color
*   glass bottle of *My Merry* nail polish
*   glass bottle of *My Merry* nail polish remover
*   glass bottle of *My Merry* toe nail polish
*   cotton poking through in cardboard base labeled "cotton puller"

Notes:
None

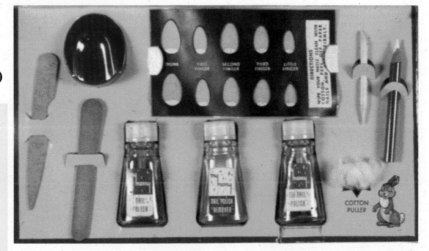

MANICURE
"Just Like Mommy's"

YEAR: **1955**
STOCK NUMBER: **11**
PRICE: **25¢**
SIZE: **3-1/2in (8.9cm) x 3-1/2in (8.9cm) x 3/4in (1.9cm)**

KNOWN CONTENTS:
- wooden emery board
- blue wooden cuticle pencil
- wooden cuticle tool
- glass bottle of *My Merry* nail polish
- 2 wooden cotton swabs
- cotton ball in hole

Notes:
None

YEAR: **1955**
STOCK NUMBER: **unknown**
PRICE: **unknown**
SIZE: **4-1/4in (10.8cm) x 3-1/4in (8.3cm) x 3/4in (1.9cm)**

KNOWN CONTENTS:

- glass bottle of *My Merry* shampoo
- yellow plastic comb
- glass bottle of *My Merry* wave set
- 3 plastic hair curlers
- *Sta Rite* pins

Notes:
The smallest of the early/mid 1950's sets.

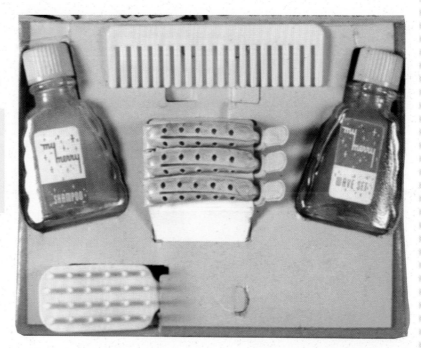

SHAVING SET
"Just Like Dad's!"

YEAR: **1955**
STOCK NUMBER: **55**
PRICE: **39¢**
SIZE: **4-1/2in (11.4cm) x 4-1/4in (10.8cm) x 7/8in (2.2cm)**

KNOWN CONTENTS:

- yellow plastic razor
- cardboard box of *GEM* razor blades
- wooden soap dish with embossed bar of soap
- red wooden shaving brush with white bristles
- glass bottle of *My Merry* after shave lotion

Notes:
None

YEAR: **1956**
STOCK NUMBER: **336**
PRICE: **39¢**
SIZE: **4-1/2in (11.4cm) x 4-1/2in (11.4cm) x
7/8in (2.2cm)**

KNOWN CONTENTS:
- cardboard can of *My Merry* "Sore Foot Powder"
- metal can of *Johnson & Johnson* "Red Cross" waterproof tape
- 3 individually-wrapped *Band-Aid* cloth strips
- wooden cotton swab
- glass bottle of *Merry Chrome*
- paper-wrapped bar of *Lifebuoy* soap
- glass bottle of *My Merry* "Sniff Salts"

Notes:
This is very similar to the first aid kit offered in 1956 except for the absence of cotton and the brand of soap. Obviously, an attempt to cater to boys.

DOLLY'S FIRST AID

YEAR: **1956**
STOCK NUMBER: **unknown**
PRICE: **39¢**
SIZE: **7in (17.8cm) x 4-1/2in (11.4cm)
x 7/8in (2.2cm)**

KNOWN CONTENTS:

- 2 wooden cotton swabs
- box of *Johnson & Johnson* "non-sterile" cotton
- metal can of *Johnson & Johnson* "Red Cross" waterproof tape
- 2 wooden tongue depressors
- glass bottle of *Merry Chrome*
- 3 individually-wrapped *Band-Aid* cloth strips
- paper-wrapped bar of *Ivory* soap
- glass bottle of *My Merry* "Sniff Salts"
- *Johnson & Johnson* junior size-plain pad

Notes:
The box has a small die-cut place marked "FOR USED COTTON"

My Merry Sets of the Mid to Late 1950's

(1957-1959)

In 1957, the *My Merry* text logo changed from black script to a more modern, 1950's style of writing. The script itself and the style of printing is unique to the line of *My Merry* toys. This style lasted from 1957 through 1959.

The 1959 catalog itself is quite a mix of items. The short-lived *My Merry* logo has now changed to the words included in an oval background. This would be the logo for the next five or so years. The 1959 catalog shows sets with both types of logos as well as a mix of play sets, closets, stores and hanging items. By the end of the 1950's, the pegboard rack was indeed starting to become a fixture in retail outlets.

While the 1959 catalog shows sets with both the older and newer logo, *My Merry* items with the oval logo will be shown in the next section. The checklist/price guide, however, will list all known items even those shown in more than one dealer catalog and by more than one stock number.

DOLLY'S FACIAL KIT
"Actually Cleans Vinyl, Latex and Plastic Dolls"

YEAR: **1957**
STOCK NUMBER: **88**
PRICE: **59¢**
SIZE: **8-1/2in (21.6cm) x 4-1/2in (11.4cm) x 7/8in (2.2cm)**
<u>**KNOWN CONTENTS:**</u>
* yellow plastic make-up cape
* box of *My Merry* "COTTON TAIL" cotton
* gold & silver tube of lipstick
* 3 wooden cotton swabs
* blue/white cardboard box of *Scotties* tissues
* glass bottle of *My Merry* "Dolly Cleanser"
* pink cardboard can of talc
* yellow powder puff w/small attached flower

Notes:
This 1957 set has the round-faced, wide-eyed little girl that adorns most succeeding *My Merry* sets in one form or another, along with the second generation *My Merry* logo. The *Parent's Magazine* recommendation logo is printed on the inside of the lid.

28

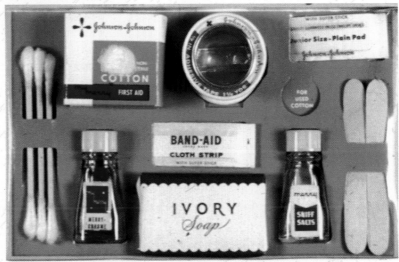

YEAR: **1957**
STOCK NUMBER: **521**
PRICE: **59¢**
SIZE: **7in (17.8cm) x 4-1/2in (11.4cm) x 7/8in (2.2cm)**
<u>KNOWN CONTENTS:</u>
- 2 wooden cotton swabs
- box of *Johnson & Johnson* "non-sterile" cotton
- metal can of *Johnson & Johnson* "Red Cross" waterproof tape
- 2 wooden tongue depressors
- glass bottle of *Merry Chrome*
- 3 individually-wrapped *Band-Aid* cloth strips
- paper-wrapped bar of *Ivory* soap
- glass bottle of *My Merry* "Sniff Salts"
- *Johnson & Johnson* junior size-plain pad

Notes:
This set is exactly the same as the COPYRIGHT 1956 set except that this version has the stock number 521:59 on the box. Inside the box lid is a small factory-applied paper sticker with **59¢** on it.

29

ELECTRIC SHAVE
"battery operated"

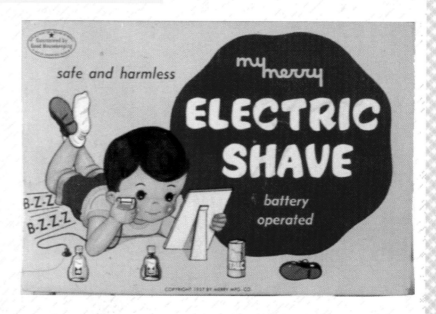

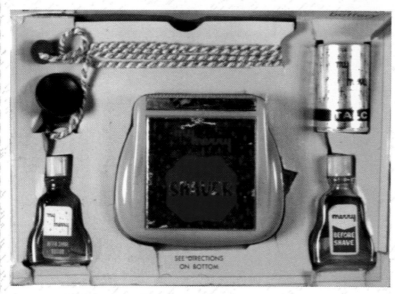

YEAR: **1957**
STOCK NUMBER: **711**
PRICE: **$1.00**
SIZE: **7in (17.8cm) x 4-3/4in (1.9cm) x 7/8in (2.2cm)**

<u>**KNOWN CONTENTS:**</u>

* two-tone rope "power cord" with suction cup and rubber plug
* cardboard canister of *My Merry* talc
* bottle of *My Merry* before shave
* blue plastic battery powered electric razor
* bottle of *My Merry* after shave

Notes:

This is the first *My Merry* set thus far with a battery powered device. The instructions on the bottom of the box describe how to remove the back of the razor (using a screwdriver) for battery insertion as well as a detailed view regarding the switch and internal buzzer. The first direction is "(1) Buy any "AA" size battery"; a far cry from the specific brand name specifications of today! The front edge of the box states "just like dad's".

YEAR: **1957**
STOCK NUMBER: **33**
PRICE: **39¢**
SIZE: **3-1/2in (8.9cm) x 3-1/2in (8.9cm) x 3/4in (1.9cm)**

KNOWN CONTENTS:
- tube of lipstick
- powder puff
- glass bottle of *My Merry* nail polish
- cardboard container of *My Merry* dusting powder

Notes:
None

RISE 'N SHINE

YEAR: **1957**
STOCK NUMBER: **415**
PRICE: **$1.00**
SIZE: **7-1/2in (19cm) x 7in (17.8cm) x 7/8in (2.2cm)**

KNOWN CONTENTS:

- red plastic toothbrush
- tube of *Pepsodent* toothpaste
- yellow cloth towel
- red plastic comb
- cardboard box of *GEM* razor blades
- wooden soap dish with yellow shaving soap (soap has relief of boy's head)
- yellow plastic razor
- red wooden shaving brush
- cardboard canister of *My Merry* talc
- glass bottle of *My Merry* men's cologne
- glass bottle of *My Merry* after shave
- paper-wrapped bar of *Lifebuoy* soap

Notes:

This is an example of a box that has suffered damage due to the product spillage. While loose powder in these sets is not a problem, the liquid has played havoc on this particular set.

YEAR: **1957**
STOCK NUMBER: **22**
PRICE: **39¢**
SIZE: **4-1/2in (11.4cm) x 3-1/2in (8.9cm)
           x 3/4in (1.9cm)**

KNOWN CONTENTS:
*   3 pink plastic hair curlers
*   red plastic hair bow
*   glass bottle of *My Merry* shampoo
*   yellow plastic hair brush
*   cardboard sheet with 5 *Sta Rite* hair pins
*   yellow plastic comb

Notes:
None.

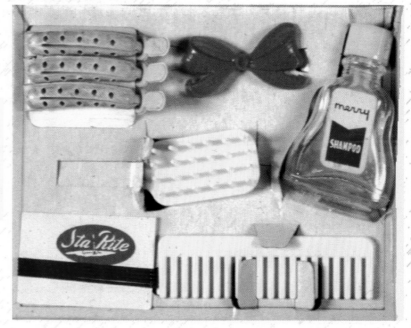

SHAVING SET

YEAR: **1957**
STOCK NUMBER: **55**
PRICE: **39¢**
SIZE: **4-1/2in (11.4cm) x 4-1/4in (10.8cm) x
7/8in (2.2cm)**

KNOWN CONTENTS:
- yellow plastic razor
- box of *GEM* razor blades
- wooden soap dish with embossed bar of soap
- red wooden shaving brush
- glass bottle of *My Merry* after shave

Notes:
None.

DOLLY'S NAIL SET
"just like mommy's"

YEAR: **1958**
STOCK NUMBER: **896**
PRICE: **69¢**
SIZE: **7-3/4in (1.9cm) x 5-1/4in (13.3cm)
        x 7/8in (2.2cm)**

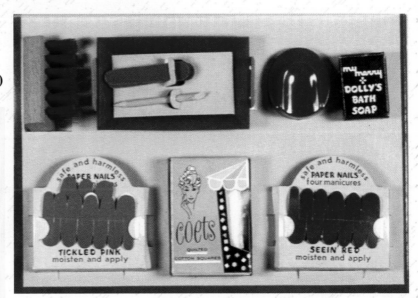

KNOWN CONTENTS:

*   red-bristle nail brush
*   red plastic soaking tray
*   3 emery boards
*   wooden cuticle tool
*   red plastic manicure finger support
*   cardboard box of *My Merry* bath soap
*   blue cardboard pack of "Tickled Pink" color paper nails
*   cardboard box of *Coets* make-up removal pads
*   blue cardboard pack of "Seein' Red" color paper nails

Notes:
None

DOLLY'S DIAPER SET
"just like mommy's"

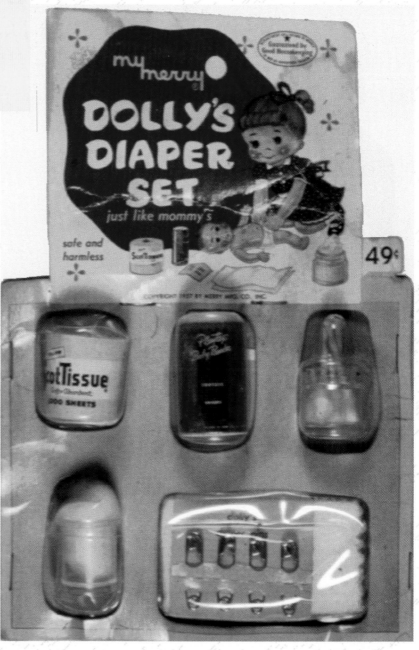

YEAR: **1957**
STOCK NUMBER: **RC-1L**
PRICE: **49¢**
SIZE: **5in (12.7cm) x 9-1/4in (10.2cm) x 3/4in (1.9cm)**
<u>KNOWN CONTENTS:</u>
- yellow roll of *ScotTissue* bathroom tissue
- 1 cardboard box *Playtex* baby powder
- plastic jar with cotton swabs
- 4 safety pins on yellow cardboard holder marked "Dolly's Diaper Pins"
- 1 cloth diaper
- plastic jar of cotton

Notes:
This set is one of ten introduced in the 1959 catalog, of which seven have the mid-1950's style graphics and logo. In many respects, this set represents an excellent compromise in merchandise packaging. The amount of cardboard is sufficient to allow colorful, eye-catching graphics. The clear plastic bubble protects and displays the contents without subjecting them to theft. The hole in the header card permits hanging and self-service. The back of this card shows five other sets, although the next set pictured in this chapter, the "Party Set", has no such printing on the rear.

YEAR: **1957**

STOCK NUMBER: **C-1**

PRICE: **49¢**

SIZE: **4-1/2in (11.4cm) x 4-1/2in (11.4cm) x 1-1/4in (3.2cm)**

KNOWN CONTENTS:

*   yellow roll of *ScotTissue* bathroom tissue
*   glass jar with cotton swabs
*   pink cardboard can of *Playtex* baby powder
*   plastic jar with cotton
*   3 linen diapers
*   yellow cardboard with 4 safety pins

Notes:

None

CLEANING CLOSET

YEAR: **1957**
STOCK NUMBER: **C-2**
PRICE: **49¢**
SIZE: **4in (10.2cm) x 5-1/2in (14cm) x
1-1/4in (3.2cm)**

KNOWN CONTENTS:

- box *Spic and Span* **or** *Soilax*
- bottle *Windex*
- cardboard can of *Dutch* cleanser
- cloth towel
- 2 rolls *ScotTowels* paper towels
- 2 sponges (these disintegrate with age)
- shammy

Notes:

This is the only set in the entire "closet" series to not have the word "Dolly" in the title. For reasons unknown, this is <u>not</u> "Dolly's Cleaning Closet", but rather, "Cleaning Closet".

YEAR: **1957**
STOCK NUMBER: **C-3**
PRICE: **$1.00**
SIZE: **6-1/4in (10.2cm) x 8in (20.3cm) x
       1-1/2in (3.8cm)**

KNOWN CONTENTS:

- 3 cloth diapers
- 2 terry towels (colors vary)
- 2 boxes *Ivory Snow* detergent
- 4 safety pins on card
- 2 terry cloth washcloths
- box blue *Dutch* cleanser
- 1 roll of *ScotTowels* paper towels
- 1 box of *Scotties* tissue
- 2 rolls of *ScotTissue* bathroom tissue, 1 blue, 1 yellow
- sponge
- 1 cardboard box *Playtex* baby powder

Notes:
None

DOLLY'S LAUNDRY CLOSET

YEAR: **1957**

STOCK NUMBER: **C-4**

PRICE: **$1.00**

SIZE: **6-1/2in (16.5cm) x 8in (20.3cm) x**
1-1/2in (3.8cm)

KNOWN CONTENTS:

- box of *Arm & Hammer Washing Soda*
- sprinkler bottle
- 2 metal hangers hanging from hole in top of box
- box of *20 Mule Team Borax*
- 4 plastic clothespins attached to box tabs
- rope clothesline
- box of *DUZ* (or *Dash*) detergent
- box of *Niagara* starch
- box of *Ivory Snow* detergent
- 2 wire sock hangers hanging from another hole in box
- white linen laundry bag
- wicker laundry basket

Notes:

None

YEAR: **1958**
STOCK NUMBER: **C-5**
PRICE: **59¢**
SIZE: **4-1/4in (10.8cm) x 5-3/4in (1.9cm) x
1-1/4in (3.2cm)**

<u>**KNOWN CONTENTS**</u>:

*   cardboard dispenser of colored cello *My Merry* party straws
*   4 wooden spoons supported from hole in top of box
*   cardboard box of *Scotkins* paper napkins
*   2 yellow plastic tumblers
*   2 white paper plates
*   red plastic ice cube tray
*   2 glass *Pepsi* bottles with metal caps

Notes:

This is one of the extra-desirable *My Merry* pieces because of the *Pepsi* products included. Devout *Pepsi* collectors would welcome the addition of this item to their collection.

DOLLY'S GUEST CLOSET

YEAR: 1958
STOCK NUMBER: C-6
PRICE: 59¢
SIZE: 4-3/4in (1.9cm) x 5-1/2in (14cm) x
1-1/4in (3.2cm)

KNOWN CONTENTS:

- pink plastic comb
- pink plastic hair brush
- roll of *ScotTissue* bathroom tissue
- yellow plastic tumbler
- red vinyl hot water bottle
- white vinyl pillow
- tan plastic *Samsonite* suitcase w/*TWA* and Paris travel stickers

Notes:
None

DOLLY'S OVER-NIGHT CLOSET

YEAR: 1958
STOCK NUMBER: C-7
PRICE: $1.00
SIZE: 8-1/2in (21.6cm) x 4-1/2in (11.4cm) x
7/8in (2.2cm)

KNOWN CONTENTS:

- cardboard "Dolly's Checker Board"
- cardboard punch-out checker set (or clear round plastic container of plastic checkers)
- yellow plastic tumbler
- 2 metal clothes hangers hanging from hole in top of box
- white vinyl pillow
- red vinyl hot water bottle
- copy of *Look* magazine
- pink flannel blanket
- red plastic glasses in white vinyl case (colors vary)
- tan plastic *Samsonite* suitcase w/*TWA* and Paris travel stickers
- red cardboard "Dolly's Hat Box"

Notes:
None

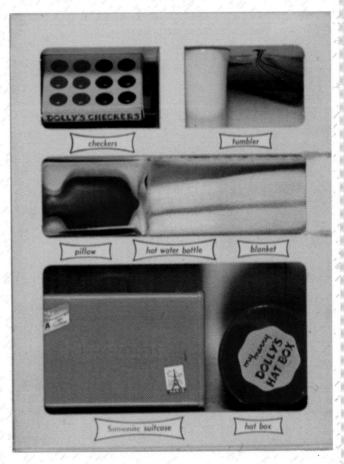

DOLLY'S HOSTESS CLOSET

YEAR: **1958**
STOCK NUMBER: **C 8**
PRICE: **$2.00**
SIZE: **7in (17.8cm) x 10in (25.4cm) x 1-1/4in (3.2cm)**
KNOWN CONTENTS:
- cardboard checker board
- clear plastic round container w/black & red checkers
- red cardboard box *Playtime* "Playing Cards"
- red pencil attached to tab in box
- white paper pad of score pads
- 4 wooden spoons in cardboard holder attached to box
- cardboard box *Scotkins* paper napkins
- 4 white paper plates
- 2 yellow plastic tumblers
- red cardboard dispenser of colored cello *My Merry* party straws
- 1 red, 2 pink balloons attached to box
- 4 round red plastic coasters in cardboard "tray"
- red plastic ice cube tray
- round red plaid metal ice bucket w/lid and red plastic handle
- yellow plastic flower vase with cloth flowers on green stems & leaves
- yellow plastic tumblers
- yellow plastic pitcher
- red rectangular plastic serving tray
- cardboard *Pepsi Cola* 6-pack with six glass, metal-capped *Pepsi* bottles

Notes:
Due to the size of this set, the weight of the contents and the number of large openings in the cardboard, it is *very* difficult to find either "Hostess Closet", red or green, in a pristine, undamaged box.

DOLLY'S BATH CLOSET

YEAR: **1958**
STOCK NUMBER: **C-9**
PRICE: **$1.00**
SIZE: **7in (17.8cm) x 9-3/4in (1.9cm) x 1-1/4in (3.2cm)**
<u>**KNOWN CONTENTS:**</u>

- large yellow terry cloth towel
- smaller pink terry cloth towel, both hanging from wooden dowel
- box of *Lux Flakes*
- wooden brush with red bristles
- cardboard can of *Dutch* cleanser
- 2 metal clothes hangers, leg-shaped hanging from hole in top of box
- yellow tumbler
- glass bottle of *My Merry* perfume in box cutout
- mirror and white plastic sink built into middle level of box
- sponge (disintegrates with age)
- 2 red boxes of *My Merry* "Dolly's Bath Soap"
- glass bottle of *My Merry* shampoo in box cutout
- toothbrush attached to tab in box
- box of *My Merry* dusting powder with clear lid
- 2 silver boxes of *My Merry* bath salts
- flowered dusting mitt
- pink box of *My Merry* bubble bath
- wicker waste basket
- wicker hamper

Notes:

This seems to be the only closet that actually has any permanent fixtures as part of the box itself. The two towels hang from a small wooden dowel in the upper left corner of the box while the mirror is in the center of the middle row. The formed plastic sink sits right below it in the center of the middle shelf. The type of sponge included is the orange-type often found totally disintegrated. This set, while dated 1958 as closets were, is not shown in the 1959 dealer catalog.

DOLLY'S PARTY SET
"just like mommy's"

YEAR: **1958**

STOCK NUMBER: **RC-5L**

PRICE: **49¢**

SIZE: **7in (17.8cm) x 11in (2.5cm) x 3/4in (1.9cm)**

<u>KNOWN CONTENTS:</u>
- cardboard box of *Scotkins* paper napkins
- two yellow plastic tumblers
- cardboard dispenser of colored cello *My Merry* party straws
- 4 paper plates
- 2 wooden spoons
- glass *Pepsi* bottle
- red plastic ice cube tray

Notes:
None

My Merry Sets of the Early 1960's

(1960-1962)

The Merry toys of the early 1960's, while more consistent than those of the 1950's, represent the last use of all cardboard packages. The closet series, now sporting the oval logo, has been reduced from nine to seven sets. The store series is complete and the *Miss Merry* name is now used for the first time with the five *Miss Merry* series sets in the peaked-roof boxes. The rack sets are still present, indicating that the self-service line is here to stay.

While the 1961 catalog shows some sets also featured in 1959, only *My Merry* items with the oval logo will be shown in this section. The checklist/price guide, however, will list all known items, even those shown in more than one dealer catalog and by more than one stock number.

It must be destiny that a book on *My Merry* and featuring the Merryland street scene was written and published in the state of Maryland.

BEWITCHED RING
"MAGIC"

THE ILLUSION

A friend drops a red jeweled ring into a container under cover of a magic handkerchief. The container is then sealed.

Surprise! when the container is reopened, the jewel has mysteriously changed its color.

RING

CUP AND LID   HANDKERCHIEF

INSTRUCTIONS INSIDE BOX
No. 5105

YEAR: **1960**
STOCK NUMBER: **5105**
PRICE: **39¢**
SIZE: **2in (5cm) x 3in (7.6cm) x 1-1/2in (3.8cm)**
<u>**KNOWN CONTENTS:**</u>
- white plastic cup
- red plastic lid
- 2 plastic rings
- instruction sheet
- *My Merry* logo cloth to cover trick

Notes:

This is definitely one of the most unusual *My Merry* items. The 1961 catalog shows a store display and the availability of 12 different magic tricks, six retailing at 39¢ and six at 59¢. The back of the box provides a brief description of the magic trick. Definitely a departure from the many miniature toys marketed under the Merry name.

BANK

YEAR: **1959**
STOCK NUMBER: **ST 1**
PRICE: **39¢**
SIZE: **5-1/2in (14cm) x 4-3/4in (1.9cm) x 1in (2.5cm)**
<u>KNOWN CONTENTS:</u>
- red vinyl wallet
- paper play money
- pad of play checks
- red wooden pencil
- cardboard bank "vault" with silver plastic coins

Notes:
This *My Merry* store is definitely not the easiest one to obtain, probably due to the minimum doll house play value and the fact that play money was always available separately in toy shops. Only six stores were shown in the 1959 catalog with the Bank being one of them. The series was increased to a total of eleven by 1961 with only ten being shown. The Bank was the first casualty in the store series reduction.

INFANTS SHOP

YEAR: **1959**
STOCK NUMBER: **ST 2 (3002)**
PRICE: **59¢**
SIZE: **5-1/2in (14cm) x 6-1/2in (16.5cm) x 1-1/4in (3.2cm)**

<u>KNOWN CONTENTS</u>:
* blue/white cardboard box of baby soap w/bar of soap
* set of 3 blue soft plastic ABC interlocking blocks in three sizes
* metallic-pink cardboard canister *Playtex* baby powder
* cardboard 6-page "Baby Book"
* black & white copy of *Look* magazine with a baby cover
* clear plastic jar with cotton swabs
* clear plastic jar with cotton ball (sitting in a marked, die-cut holder)
* yellow duck-shaped sponge
* yellow terry cloth *Vanta Towel* (in cardboard *Vanta* holder)
* pink terry cloth *Vanta Wash Cloth* (in cardboard *Vanta* holder)
* white plastic spoon
* red plastic divided feeding dish

Notes:
Unlike the Bank, this set was featured in both the 1959 and 1961 catalogs. Stock numbers such as ST-2 indicate 1959 issue while 3002 is indicative of those shown in the 1961 catalog.

YEAR: **1959**
STOCK NUMBER: **ST 3 (3003)**
PRICE: **59¢**
SIZE: **6-1/2in (16.5cm) x 5-3/4in (1.9cm) x 1-1/4in (3.2cm)**

KNOWN CONTENTS:
- cardboard *Sweetheart* ice cream cone box w/tan plastic cones
- cardboard box of *Chiclets* (various flavors available)
- 2 yellow plastic banana split dishes
- 2 white plastic spoons
- cardboard bubble gum box of real, colored gumballs
- cardboard napkin dispenser w/paper napkins
- cardboard dispenser of colored cello soda straws
- yellow plastic tumbler with white plastic-handled tumbler holder

Notes:
None

STATIONERY STORE

YEAR: **1959**
STOCK NUMBER: **ST 4 (3004)**
PRICE: $1.00
SIZE: **6-1/2in (16.5cm) x 8in (20.3cm) x 1-3/4in (1.9cm)**

KNOWN CONTENTS:
- 2 rolls *Tie Tie* brand gift ribbon (red, lavender)
- 4 cardboard *Tie Tie* brand gift boxes
- 2 paper envelopes
- 3 different rolls of *Tie Tie* brand wrapping paper, many styles available
- cardboard box with 5 *Eberhard Faber* colored pencils
- 1 box of *Scotch* cellophane tape
- 2 *Hallmark* mini cards mounted to yellow *Hallmark* display board
- 1 roll of paper postage stamps attached to *Hallmark* display board

Notes:
None

YEAR: **1959**
STOCK NUMBER: **ST 5 (3005)**
PRICE: **$1.00**
SIZE: **8-1/2in (21.6cm) x 6-1/4in (10.2cm) x 1-1/2in (3.8cm)**

KNOWN CONTENTS:

- silver plastic watering can
- cardboard box of *Scotts* play grass seed
- tan soft plastic shovel
- chamois cloth
- cardboard box of *Soilax*
- red plastic dustpan
- cardboard can of *Dutch* cleanser
- wooden scrub brush with red bristles
- wooden broom with tan soft plastic base and wheat-color bristles

- glass bottle of *Windex*
- pink foam sponge (disintegrates with age)
- silver plastic paint tray
- paint roller
- wooden ruler
- cardboard package *Scotch* sandpaper
- red plastic bucket with metal handle

Notes:
None

SUPERMARKET

YEAR: **1959**
STOCK NUMBER: **ST 6 (3006)**
PRICE: **$1.98**
SIZE: **10-1/2in (26.7cm) x 7-1/2in (19cm) x 1-3/4in (1.9cm)**

KNOWN CONTENTS:

- glass bottle *Windex* attached to box
- cardboard can *Morton* salt
- cardboard box *Ivory Snow*
- cardboard box *Lipton* tea bags with 1 tea bag inside
- cardboard box *Duz* detergent
- cardboard box *Lux Flakes*
- cardboard box *Sweetheart* sugar cones with 2 tan plastic ice cream cones
- green cardboard can *Pine Fresh Dutch* cleanser w/*Purex* bleach
- 2 rolls *ScotTowels* paper towels
- 2 green, 1 yellow *ScotTissue* bathroom tissue (color mix varies)
- cardboard box *Brillo Pads* w/1 *Brillo* pad
- cardboard box *Soilax*

- cardboard box *McCormick* whole dill seed
- cardboard box *McCormick* whole celery seed
- red plastic cash register
- cardboard box *20 Mule Team Borax*
- cardboard box *Arm & Hammer Sal Soda* concentrated washing soda
- cardboard box *Alcoa* foil wrap
- wooden scrub brush with red bristles
- 2 brown paper grocery bag
- wooden broom with tan plastic base with off-white bristles
- red plastic bucket with wire handle
- red foam sponge (disintegrates with age)
- cardboard box *Cut-Rite* wax paper

Notes:
This set has the greatest number of pieces of any *My Merry* set.

YEAR: 1959
STOCK NUMBER: ST 7 (3007)
PRICE: $2.00
SIZE: 7-1/2in (19cm) x 10-1/2in (26.7cm) x 1-3/4in (1.9cm)

KNOWN CONTENTS:

- square metal can of *ZBT* baby powder
- clear plastic jar with wooden cotton swabs
- red plastic divided feeding dish
- blue/white cardboard box of baby soap with real bar white soap
- gold cardboard metal-based lipstick tube
- cardboard box of *Coets* cotton squares
- square metal can of *Pic a Puff* cosmetic cotton
- cardboard box of *Farr* emery boards
- 2 yellow plastic banana split boats
- 4 tan plastic ice cream cones
- 4 white plastic spoons
- red plastic cash register

- 2 yellow plastic tumblers with white plastic handled tumbler holders
- black cardboard napkin dispenser with paper napkins
- cardboard box bubble gum dispenser with real gumballs
- cardboard box *Band-Aid* sheer strips
- glass bottle of *Merry Chrome*
- cardboard box of *Johnson & Johnson Steri-Pad* gauze pads
- metal round dispenser *Johnson & Johnson* adhesive tape

Notes:
None

HOBBY SHOP

YEAR: **1960**
STOCK NUMBER: **ST 8 (3008)**
PRICE: **59¢**
SIZE: **6in (15.2cm) x 6in (15.2cm) x 1-1/4in (3.2cm)**
KNOWN CONTENTS:
- cardboard can of 3 real *Tinkertoys* with silver plastic lid
- box of 3 pieces white chalk
- cardboard box with plastic *Revell* model missile
- cardboard box with plastic *Revell* model jet plane
- 8 cardboard paint by number cards
- white plastic paint brush w/black bristles
- cardboard can of red modeling clay
- cardboard box of red and yellow water color paint

Notes:

Due to its recognizable toy names (*Tinkertoy*, *Revell*), this set is quite desirable and more than a few were probably used as scenery on Lionel train layouts. While not shown in the 1959 catalog, this set is still found with the ST-8 set number marking, as well as 3008.

The box back shows the ten different stores available in 1960 (the Bank had been discontinued by then). Earlier store backs show a Merryland street scene with only eight stores.

58

YEAR: **1960**
STOCK NUMBER: **ST 9 (3009)**
PRICE: **$1.00**
SIZE: **8in (20.3cm) x 6-1/2in (16.5cm) x 1-3/4in (1.9cm)**

KNOWN CONTENTS:

- red plastic bucket w/wire handle and sponge
- cardboard box of *Brillo* pads
- black plastic car jack with *Gulf* logo
- shammy
- 3 small generic metal tools
- cardboard box of *My Merry* nuts and bolts
- *Gulf Klear-Shield* service paper towels
- 4 *Merryland* and USA road maps
- blue plastic *Gulf* car battery
- purple plastic *Gulf Crest* gasoline pump

Notes:

This *My Merry* store is one of the more difficult to obtain and desirable ones as it was one of the few to offer almost full play value for boys. Collectors of gasoline brand name products, notably "Gulf" collectors, have made this as expensive set to acquire. The outer wrap on this set originally kept the contents in place. These cellophane bands are rarely encountered on sets today.

JEWELRY SHOP

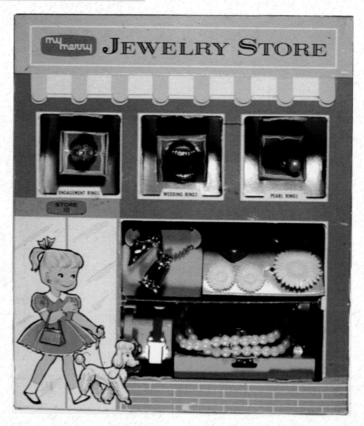

YEAR: **1960**
STOCK NUMBER: **ST 10 (3010)**
PRICE: **$2.00**
SIZE: **8-1/4in (10.2cm) x 8-1/4in (10.2cm) x 1-3/4in (1.9cm)**

<u>**KNOWN CONTENTS:**</u>

- plastic gold/diamond engagement ring set in blue cardboard display box in pink cutout
- 2 plastic wedding rings in blue cardboard display box in pink cutout
- plastic pearl ring set in blue cardboard display box in pink cutout
- silver charm bracelet with high heel shoe and railroad-type lantern on chain looped around cardboard form
- 2 red plastic clip-on heart-shaped earrings attached to cardboard form
- red plastic heart-shaped pin attached to cardboard form
- 2 yellow plastic clip-on sunflower-shaped earrings
- yellow plastic sunflower-shaped pin
- silver play watch with yellow plastic band around cardboard form
- silver play watch with red plastic band around cardboard form
- 2 silver plastic rings set in stepped cardboard form
- plastic silver and ruby ring in form
- plastic silver and emerald ring in form
- gold metal key chain-type chain on stepped form
- white plastic pearl bracelet on stepped form

Notes:
Without a doubt, this is the rarest *My Merry* shop. Fortunately, this example, the only one that the author has seen, is near perfect and complete. The colors, combined with the contents and the way that they are displayed makes this a very aesthetically pleasing and desirable set in addition to its great rarity.

60

YEAR: 1960

STOCK NUMBER: ST 11 (3011)

PRICE: $1.98

SIZE: 10-1/2in (26.7cm) x 7-1/2in (19cm) x 1-3/4in (1.9cm)

KNOWN CONTENTS:

- white box of *Coty* dolly's play eye shadow
- round cardboard box of *Coty* face powder
- white box of *Coty* dolly's emery boards
- glass bottle of *Coty* play make-up
- 2 boxes with glass bottle of *Coty* play nail polish (Merry Pink)
- box with glass bottle of *Coty* play nail polish remover
- round cardboard box of *Coty L'Aimant* dusting powder w/pink puff
- round cardboard can of *Coty L'Aimant* play talc
- box with glass bottle of *Coty L'Aimant* play cologne
- box with glass bottle of *Coty L'Aimant* bath water
- cardboard tube *Coty L'Aimant* solid pomade "Twistick"
- box with glass bottle *Coty L'Aimant* play beauty soap
- square metal can of *Pic a Puff* cosmetic cotton
- blue cardboard open box with 2 pink cotton balls
- 2 red/white cardboard tubes wax lipstick

Notes:
None

61

DOLLY'S DIAPER CLOSET
"like mom's"

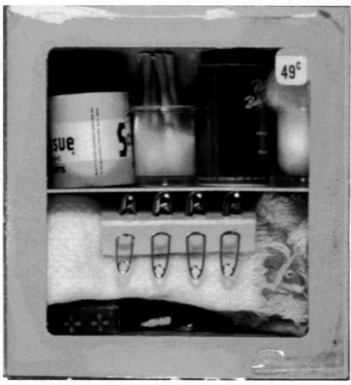

YEAR: **1960**
STOCK NUMBER: **2001 (C-1)**
PRICE: **49¢**
SIZE: **4-1/2in (11.4cm) x 4-1/2in (11.4cm) x 1-1/4in (3.2cm)**

KNOWN CONTENTS:
*   yellow roll of *ScotTissue* bathroom tissue
*   glass jar with cotton swabs
*   cardboard can of *My Merry* talc
*   plastic jar with cotton
*   3 linen diapers
*   yellow cardboard with 4 safety pins
*   box of *My Merry* soap
*   pink terry cloth towel

Notes:
This set has an unusual clear plastic cover glued over the opening where the contents are. To date, this is one of the few sets that appear to have this anti-theft device. Only seven closet sets are shown in the 1961 catalog and all seven are shown on the box back of this series of Closets. The author has acquired all seven.

YEAR: **1960**
STOCK NUMBER: **C-2 (2002)**
PRICE: **49¢**
SIZE: **4in (10.2cm) x 5-1/2in (14cm) x 1-1/4in (3.2cm)**

KNOWN CONTENTS:
- box *Spic and Span* **or** *Soilax*
- bottle *Windex*
- cardboard can of *Dutch* cleanser
- cloth towel
- 2 rolls *ScotTowels* paper towels
- 2 sponges (these disintegrate with age)
- shammy
- red plastic bucket

Notes:
Even in this later 1960 series set, the word "Dolly" is not used in the name of the set. It is rare to find this set with even a partial sponge intact. In fact, the sponge remains usually must be wiped from the box before display.

63

DOLLY'S LINEN CLOSET
"like mom's"

YEAR: **1960**
STOCK NUMBER: **C-3 (2003)**
PRICE: **$1.00**
SIZE: **6-1/4in (10.2cm) x 8in (20.3cm) x
1-1/2in (3.8cm)**

KNOWN CONTENTS:

- 2 boxes of *Scotties* tissue
- 2 rolls of yellow *ScotTissue* bathroom tissue
- white cloth washcloth
- 7 pink terry cloth diapers
- 8 safety pins on 2 cards, both cards "tabbed" onto box back
- 2 rolls of *ScotTowels* paper towels
- 2 boxes *Duz* detergent
- 3 yellow terry towels
- 1 box blue *Dutch* cleanser
- 1 cardboard box *Playtex* baby powder

Notes:
This later set from 1960 has the revised graphics as do all of the closets of this era. The contents appear to be slightly different.

YEAR: **1960**
STOCK NUMBER: **C-5 (2005)**
PRICE: **59¢**
SIZE: **4-1/4in (10.8cm) x 5-3/4in (1.9cm) x 1-1/4in (3.2cm)**

KNOWN CONTENTS:
- cardboard dispenser of colored cello *My Merry* party straws
- 4 wooden spoons supported from hole in top of box
- cardboard box of *Scotkins* paper napkins
- 2 yellow plastic tumblers
- 2 white paper plates
- red plastic ice cube tray
- 2 glass *Pepsi* bottles with metal caps

Notes:
None

DOLLY'S
HOSTESS CLOSET
"like mommy's"

YEAR: **1960**
STOCK NUMBER: **C-8 (2008)**
PRICE: **$1.98**
SIZE: **7in (17.8cm) x 10in (25.4cm) x 1-1/4in (3.2cm)**

KNOWN CONTENTS:

- cardboard checker board
- clear plastic round container w/black & red checkers
- red cardboard box *Playtime* "Playing Cards"
- red pencil attached to tab in box
- white paper pad of score pads
- 4 wooden spoons
- cardboard box *Scotkins* paper napkins
- 4 white paper plates
- red cardboard dispenser of colored cello *My Merry* party straws
- 2 yellow plastic tumblers
- 1 red, 2 pink balloons attached to box
- 4 round red plastic coasters in cardboard "tray"
- red plastic ice cube tray
- round red plaid metal *Hamilton-Skotch* ice bucket w/lid and red plastic handle
- yellow plastic flower vase with cloth flowers on green stems & leaves
- yellow plastic tumblers
- yellow plastic pitcher
- red rectangular plastic serving tray
- cardboard *Pepsi Cola* 6-pack with six glass, metal-capped *Pepsi* bottles

Notes:

This later, mint green version of the Hostess Closet seems to be slightly more difficult to find than the earlier, red version. The only real difference in the set, other than box color and the later *My Merry* logo, is the fact that the plaid metal ice bucket is listed on the package front as a *Hamilton-Skotch* brand name ice bucket.

DOLLY'S KITCHEN CLOSET
"like mom's"

YEAR: **1960**
STOCK NUMBER: **2010 (C-10)**
PRICE: **59¢**
SIZE: **4-1/2in (11.4cm) x 5-1/2in (14cm) x 1-1/4in (3.2cm)**

<u>**KNOWN CONTENTS:**</u>
- 2 yellow plastic tumblers
- 2 red coffee cups hanging from slots inside top shelf
- 2 white plastic plates
- cardboard salt & pepper shakers sitting inside blue cardboard holder marked "SALT" and "PEPPER"
- wooden-handled foam scrubber (foam is almost always deteriorated)
- cardboard box of *Jack Frost* cane sugar tablets
- yellow cardboard cookie jar with red plastic lid
- cardboard box of *DUZ* detergent (or *Tide*)

Notes:
This closet is one of the hardest to find, yet contains no real desirable, unique pieces that cannot be found in other sets. Maybe this explains its apparent lack of popularity. The back of this set also shows the seven available closets. The title of the box back reads "Dolly's Closets, just like mommy's". However. each closet is shown without "Dolly" in the title. The closets are shown in the following order: "Cleaning Closet", "Toy Closet", "Linen Closet", "Party Closet", "Hostess Closet" (mint green version), "Kitchen Closet", "Diaper Closet".

YEAR: 1960
STOCK NUMBER: C-11 (2011)
PRICE: $1.00
SIZE: 6-1/4in (10.2cm) x 8in (20.3cm) x 1-1/4in (3.2cm)
KNOWN CONTENTS:
- cardboard checker board
- clear plastic round container w/black & red checkers
- red wooden *Duncan* yo-yo with gold logo
- cardboard *Tinkertoy* canister with several small *Tinkertoys* inside
- cardboard box with plastic *Revell* model missile
- cardboard box with plastic *Revell* model jetplane
- cardboard box of *My Merry* white chalk
- cardboard canister red modeling clay
- cardboard canister blue modeling clay
- 8 cardboard paint-by-number sheets
- red plastic paint brush with black bristles
- cardboard pallet with yellow and red water color paints
- box of *Parker Bros.* Funcards with 8 color cardboard puzzles
- red plastic bucket w/wire handle
- tan soft plastic shovel
- 4 cardboard framed puzzles
- *Scrabble for Juniors* game
- plastic car or truck

Notes:
With the amount of name-brand miniature toys included, this set is one of the most desirable to toy and miniature collectors alike.

BEAUTY SHOP
"just like mommy's"

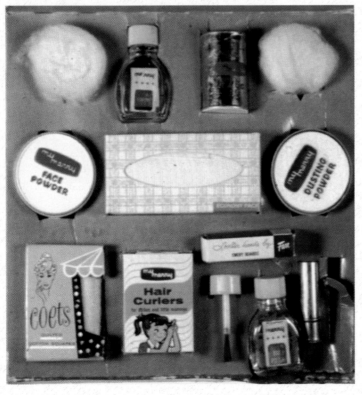

YEAR: **1960**
STOCK NUMBER: **231**
PRICE: **$1.00**
SIZE: **6-3/4in (1.9cm) x 6-3/4in (1.9cm) x 7/8in (2.2cm)**

KNOWN CONTENTS:
- 2 yellow makeup puffs
- glass bottle of *Merry* perfume
- cardboard can of *My Merry* talc
- cardboard box of *My Merry* face powder
- yellow cardboard box of *Kleenex* tissue
- cardboard box of *My Merry* dusting powder
- cardboard box of *Coets* cotton squares
- cardboard box of *My Merry* hair curlers
- cardboard box of *Farr* emery boards
- yellow plastic nail polish bottle brush
- glass bottle of *Merry* nail polish
- glass bottle of *Merry* nail polish remover

Notes:
This is one of the larger of the older sets, both in box size and number of items included.

YEAR: **1960**
STOCK NUMBER: **88 (or 1088)**
PRICE: **59¢**
SIZE: **8-1/2in (21.6cm) x 4-1/2in (11.4cm) x 7/8in (2.2cm)**

KNOWN CONTENTS:
- glass bottle of *My Merry* "Dolly Cleanser"
- cardboard box of *Wash 'n Dri* moist towelettes
- yellow/brown cardboard box of *Scotties* tissues
- yellow puff, no flower
- cardboard can of *My Merry* face powder
- glass bottle of *Merry* hand lotion
- pink cardboard box of *Coets* make-up removal pads

Notes:
Of the three different Facial Sets, this one has no make-up cape nor swabs and is the first facial set to include the name-brand *Coets*. A cellophane band around the box bottom holds the items in place. The front edge of the box states "Safe and Harmless" and shows the *Parent's Magazine* recommendation logo.

71

ELECTRIC SHAVE
"like dad's"

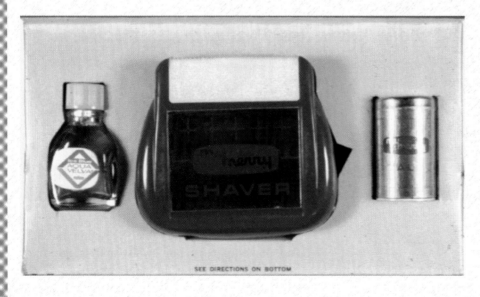

YEAR: **1957**
STOCK NUMBER: **711**
PRICE: **$1.00**
SIZE: **6-1/2in (16.5cm) x
3-1/2in (8.9cm) x
1in (2.5cm)**

KNOWN CONTENTS:
*   glass bottle of *Aqua Velva* after shave
*   red plastic battery powered electric razor
*   cardboard canister of *My Merry* talc

Notes:
None

YEAR: 1960
STOCK NUMBER: 1033
PRICE: 39¢
SIZE: 3-1/2in (8.9cm) x 3-1/2in (8.9cm) x 3/4in (1.9cm)

KNOWN CONTENTS:
- tube of lipstick
- powder puff
- glass bottle of *Merry* perfume
- cardboard container of *My Merry* face powder

Notes:
None

MANICURE
"like mom's"

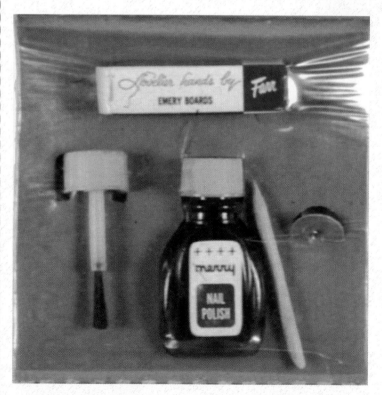

YEAR: **1960**
STOCK NUMBER: **1011**
PRICE: **29¢**
SIZE: **3-1/2in (8.9cm) x 3-1/2in (8.9cm) x 7/8in (2.2cm)**

KNOWN CONTENTS:
- cardboard box of *Farr* emery boards
- spare yellow plastic bottle brush cap
- glass bottle of *Merry* nail polish
- wooden cuticle tool

Notes:
None

YEAR: **1960**
STOCK NUMBER: **1415**
PRICE: **$1.00**
SIZE: **7in (17.8cm) x 7in (17.8cm) x 7/8in (2.2cm)**

<u>**KNOWN CONTENTS:**</u>

• box of *Aqua Velva* with bottle inside
• wooden soap dish with yellow shaving soap (soap has relief of boy's head)
• box of *GEM* razor blades
• cardboard canister of *My Merry* talc
• red wooden shaving brush
• red plastic razor
• bottle of *Merry* shampoo
• 2 bottles of after shave
• box of *Band-Aid* "Stars 'n Stripes" bandages

Notes:
None

SHAMPOO SET
"like Mommy's"

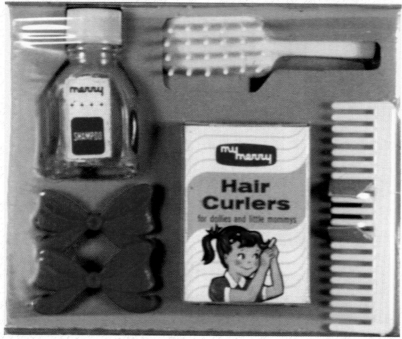

YEAR: **1960**
STOCK NUMBER: **1022**
PRICE: **39¢**
SIZE: **4-1/2in (11.4cm) x 3-1/2in (8.9cm) x 7/8in (2.2cm)**

KNOWN CONTENTS:
- bottle of *Merry* shampoo
- yellow plastic hair brush
- 2 red plastic hair bows
- box of *My Merry* hair curlers
- yellow plastic comb

Notes:
None

YEAR: **1960**
STOCK NUMBER: **1055**
PRICE: **39¢**
SIZE: **4-1/2in (11.4cm) x 3-1/2in (8.9cm) x 7/8in (2.2cm)**

KNOWN CONTENTS:

- red plastic razor
- cardboard box of *GEM* play razor blades
- wooden soap dish with embossed soap
- box of *Band-Aid* "Stars 'n Strips" bandages
- red wooden shaving brush

Notes:

This set is very similar to the 1957 offering with the exception that the after shave of 1957 has been replaced with the *Band-Aid* bandages.

DOLLY'S OUTDOOR SET

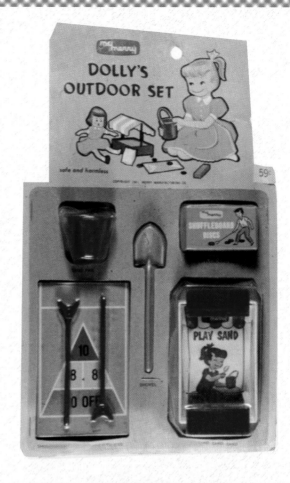

YEAR: **1961**
STOCK NUMBER: **4775**
PRICE: **59¢**
SIZE: **6-3/4in (17.1cm) x 10-1/2in (26.7cm) x
3/4in (1.9cm)**

KNOWN CONTENTS:

- red plastic sand pail
- tan plastic sand shovel
- cardboard box of *My Merry* shuffleboard discs
- cardboard shuffleboard court
- two red plastic shuffleboard pushers
- white plastic sand box with red seats
- bag of *My Merry* play sand

Notes:
None

DOLLY'S GIFT WRAP SET

YEAR: **1959**
STOCK NUMBER: **R591L (4591)**
PRICE: **59¢**
SIZE: **5in (12.7cm) x 9-1/4in (10.2cm) x
3/4in (1.9cm)**

KNOWN CONTENTS:

- 2 white/gold gift boxes
- cardboard box of *Scotch* cellophane tape
- rolls of *Tie Tie* brand gift ribbon (red)
- 2 different rolls of *Tie Tie* brand wrapping paper, many styles available

Notes:
These Rack Sets are found with both four-digit stock numbers and five-digit "RL" series.

PICNIC SET

YEAR: **1961**
STOCK NUMBER: **4771**
PRICE: **59¢**
SIZE: **8-1/4in (10.2cm) x 9-1/4in (10.2cm) x**
   3/4in (1.9cm)

KNOWN CONTENTS:
- cardboard box of *My Merry* hot dogs
- cardboard box *Alcoa* foil wrap
- paper bag of *My Merry* play charcoal
- 6 red/white checkered paper plates
- blue plastic steak grill
- 2 red/white checkered cloth napkins
- 2 red/white checkered cloth tablecloths

Notes:
None

SHAMPOO SET

YEAR: 1960
STOCK NUMBER: **R22L (4022)**
PRICE: 59¢
SIZE: **6in (15.2cm) x 7in (17.8cm) x**
   3/4in (1.9cm)

KNOWN CONTENTS:
- yellow plastic comb
- yellow plastic brush
- glass bottle of *My Merry* shampoo
- red plastic hair barrette
- cardboard box of hair curlers

Notes:
A smaller, carded version of the large shampoo sets.

TEA SET

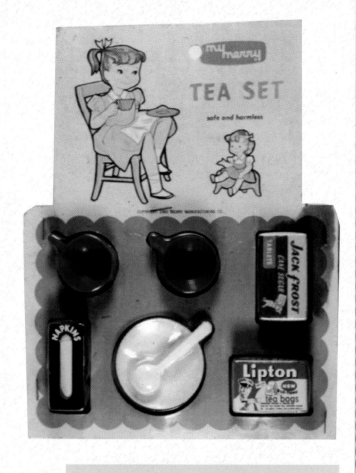

YEAR: **1960**
STOCK NUMBER: **R602L (4602)**
PRICE: **59¢**
SIZE: **7in (17.8cm) x 9in (22.9cm) x 3/4in (1.9cm)**

KNOWN CONTENTS:

- 2 red plastic coffee cup
- cardboard box of *Jack Frost* cane sugar tablets
- black cardboard box of napkins
- 2 white plastic plates
- white plastic spoons
- cardboard box of *Lipton* tea

Notes:
None

MISS MERRY AT A BAR-B-QUE

YEAR: **1961**
STOCK NUMBER: **6261**
PRICE: **59¢**
SIZE: **6in (15.2cm) x5in (12.7cm) x
2-1/4in (10.2cm)**

KNOWN CONTENTS:

- paper bag of *My Merry* play charcoal
- blue plastic steak grill
- orange plastic cookout grill w/metal grid
- cardboard box of *My Merry* red vinyl hot dogs
- 2 yellow & white check cloth napkins

Notes:
None

YEAR: **1961**
STOCK NUMBER: **6262**
PRICE: **59¢**
SIZE: **6in (15.2cm) x5in (12.7cm) x 2-1/4in (10.2cm)**

KNOWN CONTENTS:

- cardboard wall map of U.S.
- white plastic eyeglasses mounted to box
- *Miss Merry* storybook
- yellow plastic student chair
- yellow plastic student desk

Notes:
None

MISS MERRY GIVES A TEA PARTY

YEAR: **1961**
STOCK NUMBER: **6263**
PRICE: **$1.00**
SIZE: **9in (22.9cm) x 6in (15.2cm) x 2-1/4in (10.2cm)**

<u>KNOWN CONTENTS:</u>
- blue plastic chair
- red plastic tea cart with white wheels
- blue plastic teapot, sugar bowl and creamer on red cardboard holder
- 2 white plastic plates on red cardboard holder (under cart)
- 2 orange plastic cups w/handles, hanging from top of box liner
- cardboard box of *Jack Frost* sugar w/paper wrapped sugar cube
- 2 blue plastic spoons attached to inner box liner
- 2 red/white checked cloth napkins tucked into box liner
- cardboard box *Lipton* tea bags w/tea bag wrapper inside

Notes:
None

MISS MERRY PLAYS OUTSIDE

YEAR:
STOCK NUMBER: **6264**
PRICE: **$1.00**
SIZE: **9in (22.9cm) x 6in (15.2cm) x 2-1/4in (10.2cm)**

KNOWN CONTENTS:

- blue vinyl tent with green cardboard bottom
- pink flannel bedroll with yellow plastic belt-tie
- white plastic sandbox with red seats
- envelope of *My Merry* play sand
- cardboard box of wood shuffleboard discs
- 2 red plastic shuffleboard sticks
- red plastic pail with wire handle
- tan plastic shovel
- cardboard shuffleboard

Notes:
None

MISS MERRY HAS A PICNIC

YEAR: **1961**
STOCK NUMBER: **6265**
PRICE: **$1.00**
SIZE: **9in (22.9cm) x 6in (15.2cm) x 2-1/4in (10.2cm)**

<u>**KNOWN CONTENTS:**</u>

- orange plastic cookout grill w/legs and wire grate
- blue plastic steak grill hanging from hole in box
- black w/orange handles utensils: spatula, fork, grate scraper
- cloth red/white check picnic blanket
- yellow vinyl w/white sponge cooking mitt
- cardboard box of *My Merry* red vinyl hot dogs
- paper envelope of *My Merry* play charcoal
- cardboard box *Alcoa* foil wrap
- 2 red/white check cloth napkins
- 4 red/white check paper plates

Notes:
None

My Merry Sets of the Mid 1960s

(1963-1966)

The 1963 *My Merry* dealer catalog shows some fascinating Merry toys that are in slight contrast to theme. There are five sets shown and two hanging rack sets. To date, the author has seen only three of these sets. The *Skipper®* sets were not introduced until 1965 and are not shown in this catalog.

Curiously, the set packaging has evolved a bit as well. While there are play sets of various types, most are in cardboard boxes and are packed in plastic trays with a clear window. Boxes were either taped or glued shut, requiring some box damage during entry. The *Barbie®* sets were shrink wrapped, possibly at the request of Mattel. This permitted complete viewing while reducing pilfering in the stores. Some boxes had a built in handle, which permitted a larger package size without requiring an increase in the set contents.

The *Miss Merry* name is now used more prominently on many sets. By 1963, the *Miss Merry* sets packaged in the peaked-roof boxes had been discontinued. The rack sets were combinations of bubble blister cards with cardboard covers as offered previously. They were quite attractive packages, actually. This period, until 1967, basically saw the last of the boxed and cardboard supported rack cards. This was also the end of the line for the majority of name-brand products. From 1967 on, sets were primarily plastic pieces simply laid on a cardboard header card and covered with a clear plastic bubble.

BARBIE®
GLAMOUR COSMETICS
with Make-Believe Cosmetics
"for a date with Ken®"

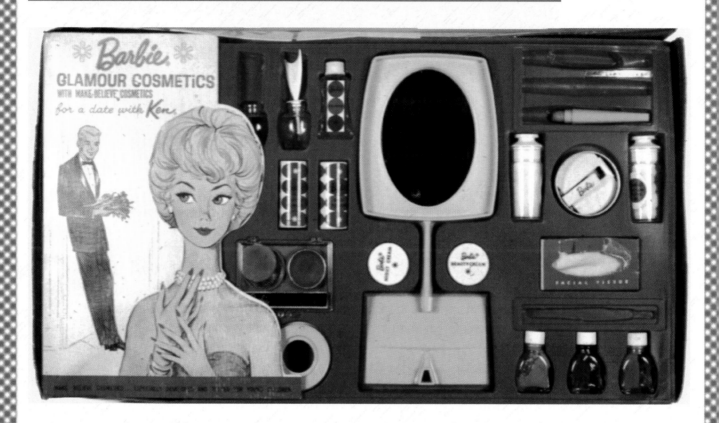

YEAR: **1963**
STOCK NUMBER: **1127**
PRICE: **$3.98**
SIZE: **17in (17.8cm) x 11in (2.5cm) x 3in (7.6cm)**
(Made by Merry Mfg. for Mattel's *Barbie®* doll)

KNOWN CONTENTS:

- two bottles of perfume with fancy white caps
- glass bottle of *Barbie®* cologne
- yellow plastic make-up mirror and base
- three lipstick applicators
- cardboard canister of *Barbie®* dusting powder
- cardboard canister of *Barbie®* bath powder
- 2 clear plastic jars of *Barbie®* cotton puffs
- *Barbie®* powder puff in cardboard tin
- clear plastic snap open box of make-up w/ 2 colors
- white plastic jars of *Barbie®* night cream
- white plastic jars of *Barbie®* beauty cream
- cardboard box of *Barbie®* facial tissue
- yellow plastic cuticle tool
- three bottles of *Barbie®* nail polish

Notes:

This set is large and rare, in both the *Barbie®* and *My Merry*-collecting worlds. The rarity and tie-in to Mattel's fashion doll makes this set the most valuable *My Merry* play set produced.

BARBIE®
Make-Believe
ROUGE AND POWDER
"for a date with Ken®"

YEAR: **1962**
STOCK NUMBER: **1124**
PRICE: **$1.00**
SIZE: **8-1/2in (21.6cm) x 4-1/2in (11.4cm) x 7/8in (2.2cm)**
(Made by Merry Mfg. for Mattel's *Barbie®* doll)

<u>KNOWN CONTENTS:</u>
- tube of lipstick
- cardboard box of *Barbie®* cotton balls
- cardboard box of *Barbie®* powder puffs
- circular can of *Barbie®* rouge
- 2 bottles of *Barbie®* face powder

Notes:
None

SKIPPER®'S PARTY CLOSET

YEAR: **1964**
STOCK NUMBER: **2001**
PRICE: **$1.00**
SIZE: **8-1/2in (21.6cm) x 4-1/2in (11.4cm) x 7/8in (2.2cm)**
(Made by Merry Mfg. for Mattel's *Skipper*® doll)

KNOWN CONTENTS:

- 2 yellow (or white) plastic bowls
- blue plastic spoon
- 2 red plastic tumblers
- purple (or orange)plastic pitcher
- cardboard box of yellow *Northern* paper napkins
- cardboard record player records
- cardboard and plastic record player

- sponge birthday cake with "Happy Birthday *Skipper*®" sticker
- cardboard box of *Skipper*® birthday candles
- blue (or orange) plastic cake cover
- pad of paper invitations
- cardboard box of *Skipper*® paper straws
- white plate

Notes:
None

88

YEAR: **1964**
STOCK NUMBER: **2002**
PRICE: **$1.00**
SIZE: **8-1/2in (21.6cm) x 4-1/2in (11.4cm) x 7/8in (2.2cm)**
(Made by Merry Mfg. for Mattel's *Skipper®* doll)

KNOWN CONTENTS:

- 3 shoe boxes
- shoe cloth
- box *Coets* make-up removal pads
- 2 rolls *Northern* tissue
- 2 towels (1 pink, 1 blue)
- blanket (fills entire box compartment)

- cardboard box of *All* detergent
- sponge
- cardboard box of *Skipper®* starch
- roll of *Northern* towels
- cardboard box of *Lux* Flakes
- red plastic dustpan

Notes:
None

SKIPPER®'S BATH CLOSET

YEAR: **1964**
STOCK NUMBER: **2003**
PRICE: **$1.00**
SIZE: **8-1/2in (21.6cm) x 4-1/2in (11.4cm) x 7/8in (2.2cm)**
(Made by Merry Mfg. for Mattel's *Skipper®* doll)

KNOWN CONTENTS:
- 2 glass bottles of shampoo
- box of *Skipper®* hair pins
- cardboard box of *Skipper®* cotton swabs
- box of *My Merry* dusting powder
- white plastic tube of lipstick
- cardboard box of *Skipper®* bath salts
- hair comb/brush
- 2 plastic jars of cotton
- *Skipper®* make-up bar (cardboard inset with mirror, fills entire compartment)
- cardboard box of *Skipper®* bath towels
- box of *Skipper®* emery boards
- flower-shaped sponge
- box of *Skipper®* beauty soap

Notes:
None

BEAUTY SLEEP
"make believe cosmetics"

YEAR: 1962
STOCK NUMBER: 1107
PRICE: **59¢**
SIZE: **5in (12.7cm) x 6-1/2in (16.5cm) x
1-1/2in (3.8cm)**

KNOWN CONTENTS:
- white cotton cloth
- cardboard box of *Gayla* bobby pins
- glass bottle of *Miss Merry's* hand lotion
- white plastic comb with handle
- white plastic container of *Miss Merry's* play beauty cream
- cardboard box of *Curity* cotton balls
- white plastic container of *Miss Merry's* play bedtime cream

Notes:

The back of this rectangular box has a letter from *Miss Merry* to Mom, Dad, Grandma and Aunt Sue:

"This exciting toy is one of my make believe cosmetic sets, especially developed and tested to give little glamour girls all the fun and excitement of "making up". Naturally, I've used only quality ingredients.

I send a gift every month to the child writing the best letter on "Why I like Miss Merry's toys." Include with the letter my picture cut out from the front of this box. Write, Miss Merry, Merry Mfg. Co., Cincinnati 15, Ohio.

You'll find more of my toys at your favorite toy counters—children love them.

Merrily yours,
Miss Merry"

This request for a cut out may explain the demise of many boxes. The back of the box also shows a "Miss Merry's Pretty Lips 'n Fingertips" and "Miss Merry's Pretty Hair".

GLAMOUR NAILS
"make believe cosmetics"

YEAR: **1962**

STOCK NUMBER: **1108-59**

PRICE: **59¢**

SIZE: **7-1/2in (19cm) x 5in (12.7cm) x 3/4in (1.9cm)**

KNOWN CONTENTS:
- 10 white plastic finger nails
- white plastic nail polish brush
- glass bottle of pink *Miss Merry's* play polish
- white cotton ball
- glass bottle of red *Miss Merry's* play polish
- tube of *Miss Merry's* play nail cream

Notes:

The back of this trapezoid-shaped box has a letter from *Miss Merry* to Mom, Dad, Grandma and Aunt Sue: All of the sets in this series have a variation of this letter.

This is one of the only sets to include a <u>tube</u> of product, similar to that of toothpaste.

POWDER 'N PERFUME
"make believe cosmetics"

YEAR: **1962**
STOCK NUMBER: **1114**
PRICE: **$1.00**
SIZE: **6in (15.2cm) x 8-1/2in (21.6cm) x 1-1/2in (3.8cm)**

KNOWN CONTENTS:
- 2 glass bottles of *Miss Merry's* "Little Flirt" perfume
- round pink cardboard box of peach blossom dusting powder
- 2 pink powder puffs
- darker, smaller pink cardboard box of "Apple Blossom" face powder
- cardboard cologne stick
- clear plastic cotton ball canister with white lid and white cotton
- cardboard box of *Miss Merry's* play talc
- clear plastic cotton ball canister with white lid and pink cotton

Notes:
The back of this trapezoid-shaped box has a letter from *Miss Merry* to Mom, Dad, Grandma and Aunt Sue: All of the sets in this series have a variation of this letter.

PRETTY FACE
"make believe cosmetics"

YEAR: **1962**
STOCK NUMBER: **1103**
PRICE: **39¢**
SIZE: **5-1/2in (14cm) x 4-1/2in (11.4cm) x 7/8in (2.2cm)**

KNOWN CONTENTS:
- plastic tube of lipstick
- cardboard canister of *Miss Merry* dusting powder
- cardboard canister of *Miss Merry* rouge with clear lid
- pink powder puff

Notes:
None

PRETTY HAIR
"make believe cosmetics"

YEAR: **1962**
STOCK NUMBER: **1102**
PRICE: **39¢**
SIZE: **5in (12.7cm) x 3-3/4in (1.9cm) x 7/8in (2.2cm)**

KNOWN CONTENTS:
- white plastic hair brush
- glass bottle of *Miss Merry's* "Hair Set"
- cardboard box of *Gayla* "Comfy Curlers"
- glass bottle of *Miss Merry's* "Blue Shampoo"

Notes:
None

PRETTY NAILS
"make believe cosmetics"

YEAR: **1962**
STOCK NUMBER: **1101**
PRICE: **39¢**
SIZE: **4in (10.2cm) x 5in (12.7cm) x 1in (2.5cm)**

KNOWN CONTENTS:
- *Miss Merry's* emery board
- white plastic nail polish brush
- wooden cuticle tool
- glass bottle of pink *Miss Merry's* nail polish
- glass bottle of *Miss Merry's* nail polish remover

Notes:

The back of the box has a letter from *Miss Merry* to Mom, Dad, Grandma and Aunt Sue:

"This exciting toy is one of my Make believe Cosmetic Sets, especially developed and tested to give little glamour girls all the fun and excitement of "making up". Naturally, I've used only quality ingredients.

I send a gift every month to the child writing the best letter on "Why I like Miss Merry's toys." Include with the letter my picture cut out from the front of this box. Write, Miss Merry, Merry Mfg. Co., Cincinnati 15, Ohio.

You'll find more of my toys at your favorite toy counters—children love them.

Merrily yours,
Miss Merry"

This request for a cut out may explain the demise of many boxes. The back of the box also shows a "Miss Merry's Hospital Set $1.00" and "Miss Merry's Model's Make-Up 59¢."

YEAR: 1962
STOCK NUMBER: 4104
PRICE: 39¢
SIZE: **4-1/4in (10.8cm) x**
          3-1/2in (8.9cm) x 7/8in (2.2cm)

KNOWN CONTENTS:
- tube of *Mister Merry's* play shave cream
- yellow plastic razor
- cardboard box of *Mister Merry's* paper blades

Notes:

One of the simpler sets, Slick Shave provided some play fun for little boys as well. The back of this header-carded box also has a letter from *Mister Merry* to Mom, Dad, Grandma and Aunt Sue:

"This exciting toy is one of my Make Believe Sets, especially developed and tested to give little fellas all the fun and excitement of "making up". Naturally, I've used only quality ingredients.

I send a gift every month to the child writing the best letter on "Why I like Mister Merry's toys." Include with the letter my picture cut out from the front of this box. Write, Mr. Merry, Merry Mfg. Co., 531 North Wayne, Cincinnati 15, Ohio.

You'll find more of my toys at your favorite toy counters-children live them.

Merrily yours,
Mister Merry"

The letter is very similar to the one on several *Miss Merry* sets, with a few word changes. Interestingly, a North Wayne street address is listed.

VISITING NURSE
"make believe first aid"

YEAR: **1962**
STOCK NUMBER: **1106**
PRICE: **59¢**
SIZE: **5in (12.7cm) x 6-1/2in (16.5cm) x 1-1/2in (3.8cm)**

KNOWN CONTENTS:

- 3 cotton swabs
- plastic box *Miss Merry's* bubble gum pills
- clear plastic hypodermic needle with blue plunger
- red plastic tweezers
- cardboard box of *Curity Telfa* pads
- glass bottle of *Miss Merry's* H2O
- cardboard box of *Curad* plastic bandages

Notes:
None

YEAR: **1962**
STOCK NUMBER: **3301**
PRICE: **59¢**
SIZE: **8-3/4in (1.9cm) x 5-1/4in (13.3cm) x 1in (2.5cm)**

KNOWN CONTENTS:
- cardboard box of *Chix* diapers
- pink fish-shaped bath sponge
- clear plastic drinking glass
- pink plastic baby bottle nipple/top
- red plastic baby oil cup
- cardboard baby blanket box by *Perperell*
- cardboard box of *Q-tips*
- white plastic baby bottle with pink plastic top
- cardboard box of baby soap

Notes:
Without a doubt, this is one of the two most difficult Merry Playthings sets of the era.

PLAYTHINGS For Your Dolly's Bathroom

YEAR: **1962**
STOCK NUMBER: **3302**
PRICE: **59¢**
SIZE: **8-3/4in (1.9cm) x 5-1/4in (13.3cm) x 1in (2.5cm)**

KNOWN CONTENTS:
- glass bottle of *My Merry* play mouthwash
- cardboard box of *Mr. Bubble* bubble bath
- orange sponge
- purple bar of soap (looks like two attached hexagonal nuts)
- roll of *Northern* bathroom tissue
- cardboard box of *Northern* facial tissue
- white plastic handled bath scrub brush

Notes:
This series of Playthings sets are packaged not unlike holiday candy. A sealed, cardboard box with a window displays the items, each secured in a plastic tray compartment. These sets are uncommon, as are most of the sets in this era.

YEAR: **1962**
STOCK NUMBER: **3303**
PRICE: **59¢**
SIZE: **8-3/4in (1.9cm) x 5-1/4in (13.3cm) x 1in (2.5cm)**

KNOWN CONTENTS:
- cardboard box of *Brillo* pads
- plastic container marked "sugar"
- plastic container marked "flour"
- *Better Home & Gardens* cookbook
- roll of *Northern* paper towels
- cardboard box of *Playtex* "Living Gloves" with plastic glove inside
- gray plastic pot with two small handles
- gray plastic pan with handle

Notes:
None

YEAR: **1962**
STOCK NUMBER: **3304**
PRICE: **59¢**
SIZE: **8-3/4in (1.9cm) x 5-1/4in (13.3cm) x 1in (2.5cm)**

KNOWN CONTENTS:
- cardboard box with 4 *Halo* birthday candle holders
- white plastic cake plate
- light blue plastic cake plate cover
- cardboard box of *Carnival* jumbo straws w/paper straws
- 2 yellow plastic yellow cups
- yellow foam "sponge" cake with hole in center
- cardboard box of *Halo* birthday candles
- purple plastic pitcher

Notes:
None

PLAYTHINGS
For Your
Dolly's Dining Room

YEAR: **1962**

STOCK NUMBER: **3305**

PRICE: **59¢**

SIZE: **8-3/4in (1.9cm) x 5-1/4in (13.3cm) x 1in (2.5cm)**

KNOWN CONTENTS:

- wooden salad bowl
- black plastic salad ladle
- *Bucilla Wonder-Looper Table Mats* placemats
- gray plastic knife and fork
- cardboard box of *Northern* luncheon napkins
- 2 small red plastic tumblers
- 2 green plastic bowls
- white plastic plate

Notes:

None

PLAYTHINGS For Your Dolly's Den

YEAR: **1962**
STOCK NUMBER: **3306**
PRICE: **59¢**
SIZE: **8-3/4in (1.9cm) x 5-1/4in (13.3cm) x 1in (2.5cm)**

<u>**KNOWN CONTENTS**</u>:
- cardboard box of *Merry* notes
- blue wooden pencil
- yellow cardboard *My Merry* photo album
- cardboard *Capitol Records Little Toot* record album
- purple cardboard phonograph
- paper envelope of developed *Kodak* film

Notes:
None

YEAR: **1962**
STOCK NUMBER: **3308**
PRICE: **$1.00**
SIZE: **10-3/4in (1.9cm) x 6in (15.2cm) x 1in (2.5cm)**

KNOWN CONTENTS:

- silver cardboard coffee "tin" with a few beans inside
- tan plastic cutting board
- cardboard box of *Topco* aluminum foil
- cardboard box of *Waxtex* sandwich bags
- silver serrated butcher knife
- red cardboard thermos bottle with plastic cup/lid
- cardboard box of *Waxtex* wax paper
- cardboard box of *Pepperidge Farm* bread with sponge bread inside
- orange plastic dome-type lunch box
- silver plastic coffee pot
- yellow coffee pot basket and red shaft

Notes:
This is the largest of the "Playthings" sets.

BABY MERRY
"A Dee-J paper doll for ages 3 to 7"

YEAR: **1964**
STOCK NUMBER: **4350**
PRICE: **39¢**
SIZE: **5in (12.7cm) x 9in (22.9cm) x 5/8in (20.3cm)**

KNOWN CONTENTS:
- cardboard baby paper doll
- plastic feeding bottle in die-cut background
- cardboard box of *Chix* diapers
- "12 Rub 'n Stay outfits for baby (peel off- play again)"
- Rub 'n Stay stick (crayon-looking device to help clothing stick to doll)

Notes:

An orange and black sticker on the front states that the "amazing" Rub 'n Stay stick is included in this set. It appears to be a packaging afterthought.

The back of this box shows a veritable plethora of *My Merry* items, some of which have eluded the author to this point. Three Trayette sets, "Baby", "Beauty" and "Hospital", include items to support these themes. Three Playsets, "Shavin' Stuff", "Party Glamour", and "Glamour Nails" also have corresponding contents. All six of these sets are packaged in clear window boxes with slide-out plastic trays holding the contents. Three Paper Dolls—"Miss Merry Shapely Shape", "Jodi", and "Mindy"— are in the same style as this "Baby Merry" set.

In addition to these sets, a note from *Miss Merry* reads:

"Have you heard about the Merry Pen Pal Club? If you'd like to join, send us your name, address, age and this tag to Merry, 531 North Wayne Ave., Cincinnati, Ohio 45215.

Miss Merry"

This request for yet another a cut-out may explain the demise of *My Merry* packaging.

YEAR: **1964**
STOCK NUMBER: **6403**
PRICE: **$1.00**
SIZE: **5-1/4in (13.3cm) x 19 in (48.3cm) x 1-1/2in (4cm)**

KNOWN CONTENTS:
- cardboard "Donna Reed" doll
- stick-on clothing pieces

Notes:
This is a Dee-J doll in the same series as the other four dolls following. Each is made of card stock printed with a shiny surface that permits stick-on clothing and/or hairpieces. This Donna Reed doll is quite unusual in that it is the only *My Merry* piece to reference a living person. As this book went into the editing stage, a boxed example of this *My Merry* finally surfaced! The box is unusual as well. It folds like the greeting card series with *each* half being 3/4in think and *each* half having a clear window. The paper doll was on display through the outer window (the window is above the Donna Reed script writing) and the clothing inside above "Donna Reed's Own Fashion Chart". On the left inside "cover", Donna Reed briefly describes her life as a TV mom and as the real Mrs. Tony Owen. The very back of the box shows other *My Merry* products as well as the Jo paper doll, the only *My Merry* doll of similar size to Donna Reed. The somewhat damaged box of this example shows the outside in the open position.

JO PAPER DOLL
"you can change her face"

YEAR: **1964**
STOCK NUMBER: **6502**
PRICE: **$1.00**
SIZE: **8in (20.3cm) x 18-1/2in (21.6cm) H x 1-1/2in (3.8cm)**

KNOWN CONTENTS:
- cardboard "Jo" doll
- stick-on clothing pieces

Notes:
This is a Dee-J doll. The box back shows a few other *My Merry* sets along with the most curious piece, a Donna Reed cardboard doll. The words "a Dee-J paper doll for ages 4 to 9". Unlike the "Jodi" doll, this one is nearly 15in (38cm) high in a box that tops 18in (46cm).

LISA PAPER DOLL
"comb her hair"

YEAR: **1964**
STOCK NUMBER: **4352**
PRICE: **39¢**
SIZE: **5in (12.7cm) x 8-1/2in (21.6cm) H x 3/4in (1.9cm)**

KNOWN CONTENTS:
- cardboard "Lisa" doll with "real" hair
- 20 stick-on clothing pieces

Notes:
This is a Dee-J doll. The box back shows a few other *My Merry* sets of the era.

109

JODI PAPER DOLL
"with the SHAPELY-SHAPE body"

YEAR: **1964**
STOCK NUMBER: **4362**
PRICE: **59¢**
SIZE: **6-1/2in (16.5cm) x 10in (25.4cm) H x 3/4in (1.9cm)**

KNOWN CONTENTS:
- cardboard "Jodi" doll
- 15 stick-on clothing pieces

Notes:

The box front states that "over 15 high fashion Rub 'n Stay costumes" are included. "Peel off…play again" is the slogan. "The Shapley Shape body and exclusive Dee-J process" is another touted feature. The words "a Dee-J paper doll for ages 4 to 9" is probably a giveaway that this product may have been produced for, rather than by the Merry Manufacturing Company. Obviously, a similar product to the immensely popular *Colorforms* of the period.

The back of this box shows several *My Merry* sets, including three Paper Dolls, "Miss Merry Shapely Shape", "Jodi", and "Mindy"..

In addition to these sets, a note from *Miss Merry* reads:

"Have you heard about the Merry Pen Pal Club? If you'd like to join, send us your name, address, age and this tag to Merry, 531 North Wayne Ave., Cincinnati, Ohio 45215. I'll send you a Pal's name.

Miss Merry"

MINDY PAPER DOLL
"change her hair-do"

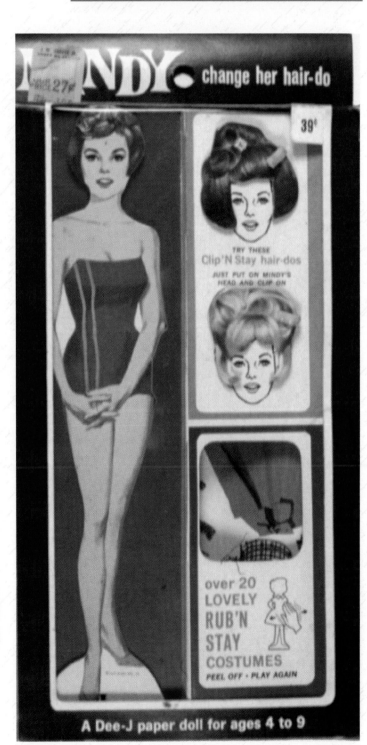

YEAR: **1964**

STOCK NUMBER: **4351**

PRICE: **39¢**

SIZE: **5in (12.7cm) x 8-1/2in (21.6cm) H x**
3/4in (1.9cm)

KNOWN CONTENTS:
- cardboard "Mindi" doll
- 2 stick-on hair pieces
- stick-on clothing pieces

Notes:

This is a Dee-J doll. The box back shows other *My Merry* sets and dolls. Although similar to Jodi, Mindy is the doll that comes with stick-on *hair* pieces rather than *clothing* items.

BRUSH-ON BEAUTY
"make believe cosmetics"

YEAR: **1965**
STOCK NUMBER: **1323**
PRICE: **$1.00**
SIZE: **8-1/2in (21.6cm) x 8-1/2in (21.6cm) x 1in (2.5cm)**

<u>**KNOWN CONTENTS:**</u>
- cardboard box of *Merry* brush-on lids brush
- open plastic container with dark blue rouge
- open plastic container with peach rouge
- cardboard box of *Merry* brush-on cheeks brush
- cardboard box of *Merry* brush-on brows brush
- open plastic container with brown rouge
- red plastic lipstick tube
- cardboard stand-up vanity with metal "mirror" attached
- blue cardboard book <u>How to Do Brush-On Lids</u>
- purple cardboard book <u>How to Do Brush-On Brows</u>
- red cardboard book <u>How to Do Brush-On Cheeks</u>

Notes:
The back of this package reads "Hello, I'm Miss Merry. Would you like to have an 8" Miss Merry Paper Doll with pretty cut-out paper clothes? If so, send 10¢ with your name, address and the number of this toy cut from the bottom of the box to me: Miss Merry, Dept. 10, Merry Mfg. Co., Cincinnati 15, Ohio. Also - you will find more *My Merry* Play Things toys and many *Miss Merry* make-believe cosmetic sets at stores everywhere - I hope you will enjoy all of them. P.S. I love you. Merrily, Miss Merry."

Also shown are six sets, "Pretty Lips 'n Finger Tips", "Party Glamour", "Brush-on Beauty", "Wake-up Make up", "Play Hospital" and Neat 'n Clean".

JODI PURSE DOLL GO-GO-TIME THEME

YEAR: 1966
STOCK NUMBER: 1703
PRICE: $1.00
SIZE: 6in (15.2cm) x 5-1/2in (14cm) H x 2-1/2in (5cm)

KNOWN CONTENTS:
- plastic purse case, clear front, yellow back with handle
- sticker on front lists features of doll, "unbreakable", etc.
- brunette-haired doll with moveable limbs, 4 fi" tall in white dress with red ric-rac trim at neck
- cardboard backdrop in pennant theme, containing stock number on bottom

Notes:
The 1967 catalog shows four dolls, each in a different-colored, circular case with a cardboard backdrop theme. This doll, circa 1966, preceded those. While the 1967 series included nameless dolls, these had names.

JUDY PURSE DOLL GO-GO-TIME THEME

YEAR: **1966**
STOCK NUMBER:**1703**
PRICE: **$1.00**
SIZE: **6in (15.2cm) x 5-1/2in (14cm) H x 2-1/2in (5cm)**

KNOWN CONTENTS:
- plastic purse case, clear front, yellow back with handle
- sticker on front lists features of doll, "unbreakable", etc.
- brunette doll with moveable limbs, 4 fi" tall in white dress with red ric-rac trim at neck
- cardboard backdrop in pennant theme, containing stock number on bottom

Notes:
Note how Jodi and Judy are essentially the same except for the name on the package. Even the stock numbers are the same.

Merry Greeting Cards

The author armed himself with four original dealer catalogs and over 160 *My Merry* items during the book layout process. While the greeting cards in this chapter have pieces from the early 1960's Merry sets, they are not pictured in any catalog. It is possible that they were not offered in toy and hobby shops but possibly through drug store and card shops instead. This could explain the lack of information in the dealer toy catalogs. In any case, enjoy these charming *My Merry* sets believed to be from the early 1960's.

BIRTHDAY WISHES ARE IN THE AIR
sides continually read Happy Birthday

YEAR: **1960's**
STOCK NUMBER: **50B-2202**
PRICE: **50¢**
SIZE: **3in (7.6cm) x 8in (20.3cm) x 3/4in (1.9cm)**

<u>KNOWN CONTENTS:</u>
*   silver cardboard tube of lipstick
*   red and white cardboard box of *Kleenex* tissues
*   blue plastic brush

Notes:
This is a get-well card for girls. The cover features a caricature of a girl in front of a mirror trying on a new dress. Inside, she is dressed and the printing states "pretty your lips 'n comb your hair". This card has a vertical, left-hinged flap as do the closets, except the flap covers the contents entirely, like a thick get-well card should. Several cards exist in this series.

TO A JEWEL OF A LITTLE GIRL
"Happy Birthday"

YEAR: **1960's**
STOCK NUMBER: **50B-2203**
PRICE: **50¢**
SIZE: **3in (7.6cm) x 8in (20.3cm) x 3/4in (1.9cm)**

<u>**KNOWN CONTENTS:**</u>
- pink plastic heart-shaped broach
- white plastic ruby ring
- plastic pearl bracelet
- silver plastic ruby ring

Notes:
None

YEAR: **1960's**
STOCK NUMBER: **50B-2204**
PRICE: **50¢**
SIZE: **3in (7.6cm) x 8in (20.3cm) x 3/4in (1.9cm)**

KNOWN CONTENTS:
- red/white checkered napkin
- cardboard box of *My Merry* hot dogs
- blue plastic hot dog cooker
- black plastic hot dog fork with red handle
- sponge cooking mit

Notes:
This is a get-well card for boys and girls. The cover features a caricature of a hot dog riding a cooking fork. Inside, a birthday party scene is shown with two caricature children. This card has a vertical, left-hinged flap as do the closets, except the flap covers the contents entirely, like a thick birthday card should.

HOT DAWG IT'S YOUR BIRTHDAY
sides show
small birthday cakes

HAPPY BIRTHDAY
sides show
small birthday cakes

YEAR: **1960's**
STOCK NUMBER: **50B-2205**
PRICE: **50¢**
SIZE: **3in (7.6cm) x 8in (20.3cm) x 3/4in (1.9cm)**

KNOWN CONTENTS:
- blue cardboard *Merry* coloring book
- 4 wooden colored pencils
- red cardboard *Merry* coloring book

Notes:
This is a birthday card for both boys and girls. The cover features large letters and a caricature of a happy rabbit. Inside, the cover reads *"Hurrah Let's Draw"* with a hand holding colored pencils. This card has a vertical, left-hinged flap as do the closets, except the flap covers the contents entirely, like a thick birthday card should.

YEAR: **1960's**
STOCK NUMBER: **50C-2301**
PRICE: **50¢**
SIZE: **3in (7.6cm) x 8in (20.3cm) x 3/4in (1.9cm)**

<u>**KNOWN CONTENTS:**</u>
- 4 watercolor paint pads
- red wooden paint brush
- 8 paint-by-number cards

Notes:

This is a get-well card for boys and girls. The cover features a caricature of a dog in front of a door with a "QUIET" sign hanging from the knob. Inside, the cover reads *"Paint away and GET WELL SOON"* with a paint-by-number theme. All three toys are from the Toy Closet. This card has a vertical, left-hinged flap as do the closets, except the flap covers the contents entirely, like a thick get-well card should.

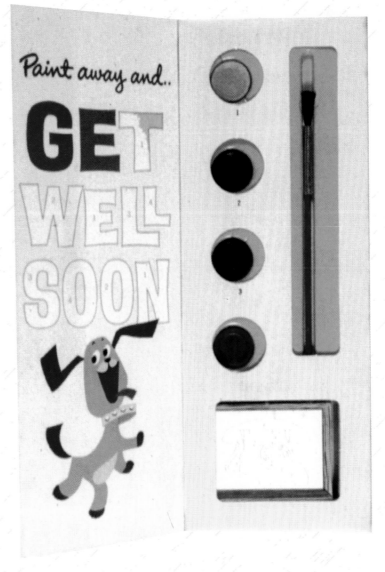

121

HOPE YOU GET WELL MIGHTY QUICK

YEAR: **1960's**
STOCK NUMBER: **50C-2302**
PRICE: **50¢**
SIZE: **3in (7.6cm) x 8in (20.3cm) x 3/4in (1.9cm)**

KNOWN CONTENTS:
- white soft plastic plate
- 2 blue plastic spoons
- 2 red plastic cups
- cardboard box *Scotkins* paper napkins

Notes:

This is a get-well card for girls. The cover features a carica-ture of a girl sick in bed with her doll. Inside, the cover reads *"It's no par 'Tea' Being Sick"* with a tea-time theme. This card has a vertical, left-hinged flap as do the closets, except the flap covers the contents entirely, like a thick get-well card should.

YEAR: **1960's**
STOCK NUMBER: **50C-2303**
PRICE: **50¢**
SIZE: **3in (7.6cm) x 8in (20.3cm) x 3/4in (1.9cm)**

KNOWN CONTENTS:
- box of *Parker Bros.* Funcards with 8 color cardboard puzzles
- 4 cardboard framed puzzles
- *Scrabble for Juniors* game

Notes:

This is a get-well card for boys. The cover features a caricature of a sick boy through a window. Inside, the cover reads *"Play a game/ while you're sick/ You'll get well/ twice as quick.* All three toys are from the Toy Closet. This card has a vertical, left-hinged flap as do the closets, except the flap covers the contents entirely, like a thick get-well card should.

YOU SICK?
AWWWW!
sides continually read
get well soon!

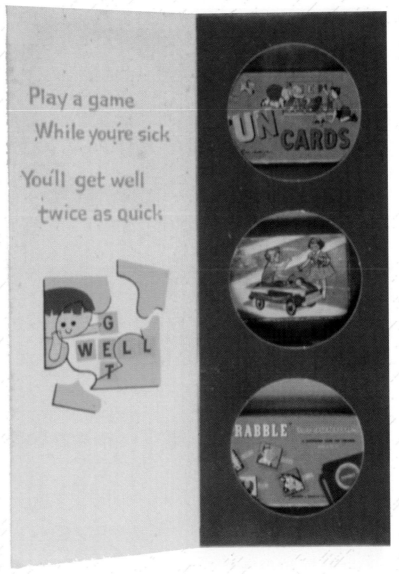

123

PERK UP, BOY!
sides continually read
PERK UP! GET WELL!

YEAR: **1960's**
STOCK NUMBER: **50C-2304**
PRICE: **50¢**
SIZE: **3in (7.6cm) x 8in (20.3cm) x 3/4in (1.9cm)**

KNOWN CONTENTS:
- cardboard box with plastic *Revell* model jet plane
- red wooden *Duncan* yo-yo with gold logo
- cardboard box with plastic *Revell* model missile

Notes:
This is a get-well card for boys. The cover features a caricature of a sick marionette, complete with medicine. Inside, the cover reads *"GET FEELIN' SNAPPY Here's tiny toys to make you happy"* with a happy marionette. All three toys are from the Toy Closet. This card has a vertical, left-hinged flap as do the closets, except the flap covers the contents entirely, like a thick get-well card should. An example of this card amazingly sold for over $400 at a 1996 auction. To date, the card that reads "Happy Birthday Little Shaver" is the only one to elude the author.

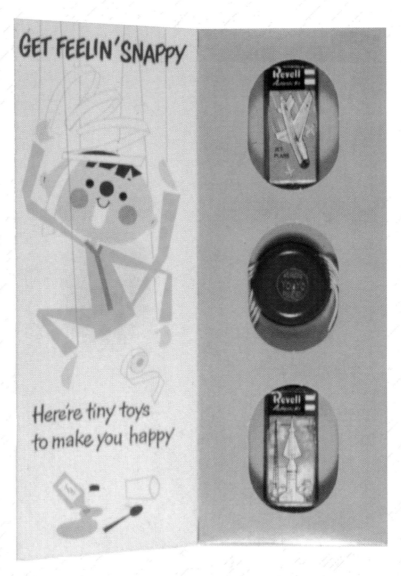

The Blister-Carded Era

(1967-1970's)

For a *My Merry* collector, the 1967 (and 1972) catalogs are quite a rude awakening. Gone is most of the charm of name brand product, realistic cardboard containers and nice packaging. Gone too, is the *My Merry* name. "Merry Toys", with several *Miss Merry* sets, have replaced the *My Merry* logo and name. While the *Merry Toys* name was indeed used longer than that of *My Merry*, the latter was chosen for this book's title since it is synonymous with the era that most collectors fancy.

With only a few exceptions, the sets from here on out will be packaged in the same manner as other inexpensive toys of the day. Play sets such as these are not mainstream playthings anymore. Children have *Barbie®*, GI Joe™, and Matchbox® cars to play with. *My Merry* sets of the 1950's and early 1960's were play entities themselves. Now, they can supplement *Barbie®* play at best, or become an inexpensive "filler" present for a child. Sets not offered on blister cards are in thin cardboard boxes and have been shrink-wrapped. In short, one era has ended and another begun.

In 1972, many of these blister-carded sets have the number of the assortment that they were offered in and do not refer to specific set names or stock numbers. In this section, sets will be grouped by year and shown alphabetically.

LET'S WASH 'N IRON

YEAR: **1966**
STOCK NUMBER: **1431**
PRICE: **$1.00**
SIZE: **8in (20.3cm) x 10in (25.4cm) x 1-1/4in (3.2cm)**
KNOWN CONTENTS:
- cardboard box of *Niagara* instant starch
- blue/white/black plastic iron
- white plastic ironing board
- cardboard box of *Rinso* detergent
- plastic *My Merry* spray bottle.
- cardboard box of *All* detergent
- orange rectangular plastic wash tub
- cloth drawstring laundry bag
- 3 plastic fashion doll clothes hangers
- *Merry* string clothesline wrapped around cardboard piece

Notes:
One of the most interesting sets in the way it is packaged. The frame-style box is similar to the way vintage fashion doll outfits were sold. This set also has a fair number of plastic pieces, as was the trend, yet three different name-brand products were included as well. The feature of this set was the "heating action" iron that achieved this feat with the addition of hot water in its tank! This set, and a few others in the same series, are a welcome addition to the simpler and cheaper sets of this era and are actually the last of their type.

YEAR: **1967**
STOCK NUMBER: **1801**
PRICE: **$1.00**
SIZE: **6in (15.2cm) x 5-1/2in (14cm) H x 2-1/2in (5cm)**
KNOWN CONTENTS:
- plastic purse case, clear front, pink back with handle, "New Pose 'n Play Body" sticker on front
- brunette-haired doll with moveable limbs, 4 fi" tall in red velvet/white lace dress
- cardboard backdrop in party theme, containing stock number on bottom

Notes:
A total of four dolls were offered in 1967, each with a different theme and color case. The others included a green school themed case, #1802, an orange go-go themed case, #1803, and a bedtime-themed case, #1804. These were produced due to obvious success with earlier offerings of Judy and Jodi in 1966. The Jodi/Judy dolls were offered in round plastic cases shaped differently from these. The Mattel "Liddle Kiddles" series of dolls did not hurt the interest in small dolls either.

HEAVENLY HAIR

YEAR: **1966**
STOCK NUMBER: **1302**
PRICE: **39¢**
SIZE: **5in (12.7cm) x 7in (17.8cm)**

KNOWN CONTENTS:
- pink plastic hair brush
- 2 yellow snap-type hair curlers
- yellow terrycloth towel with "Dolly's Towel" paper band
- glass bottle of *Merry* shampoo
- glass bottle of *Merry* wave set

Notes:
None

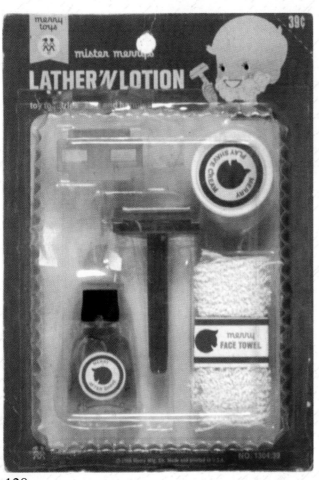

LATHER 'N LOTION

YEAR: **1966**
STOCK NUMBER: **1304**
PRICE: **39¢**
SIZE: **5in (12.7cm) x 7in (17.8cm)**

KNOWN CONTENTS:
- green plastic razor blade
- white plastic jar of *Merry* play shave cream
- red plastic safety razor
- glass bottle of *Merry* after shave lotion
- blue terry cloth face towel with paper wrapper

Notes:
None

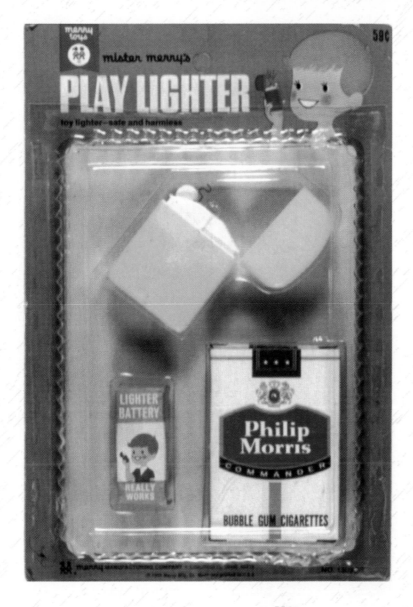

YEAR: 1966
STOCK NUMBER: 1309
PRICE: 59¢
SIZE: 6in (15.2cm) x 8-3/4in (1.9cm)

KNOWN CONTENTS:
- yellow/white plastic *Zippo*-style lighter with light bulb
- cardboard box with light battery, size N
- cardboard box of *Philip Morris* bubble gum cigarettes

Notes:
Obviously produced at a time when a child pretending to smoke cigarettes was not politically incorrect and not viewed in a negative light.

129

PLAY PRECIOUS GEMS
"Play Like Mommy"

YEAR: **1966**
STOCK NUMBER: **1602**
PRICE: **39¢**
SIZE: **6in (15.2cm) x 8in (20.3cm)**
<u>**KNOWN CONTENTS:**</u>
- clear plastic "diamond" or "ruby" necklace
- gold metal engagement-style solitaire ring
- glass bottle of *Merry* perfume
- clear plastic "diamond" or "ruby" bracelet

Notes:
None

YEAR: **1967**
STOCK NUMBER: **1632**
PRICE: **$1.00**
SIZE: **9in (5cm) x 10-1/2in (26.7cm) x 3/4in (1.9cm)**

KNOWN CONTENTS:
- 2 plastic flower clip-on earrings
- plastic bracelet with simulated white teeth
- plastic flower ring
- plastic necklace with simulated white teeth
- plastic flower pin
- cloth purse with simulated animal print
- glass bottle of "Jungle Flower" cologne

Notes:
An unusual set to say the least. The colorful cartoon jungle theme on the package is attractive and the box is of frame-type construction, not unlike fashion doll outfits of the era.

FASHION MODEL DRESS UP JEWELRY

YEAR: **1968**
STOCK NUMBER: **1653**
PRICE: **39¢**
SIZE: **9in (22.9cm) x 13in (7.6cm)**

KNOWN CONTENTS:
- blue plastic bead necklace w/large blue "jewel"
- blue plastic bead bracelet w/large blue "jewel"
- blue plastic "jewel" drop earrings
- gold metal ring with blue "stone"
- pink plastic lipstick tube
- pink plastic eyeglasses with false eyelashes attached

Notes:
The back of this package has a large, colorful scene in a late-1960's "MOD" theme with the words "Look for us, your Merry friends, in your toy store".

LITTLE FASHION QUEEN
DRESSER SET

YEAR: **1968**
STOCK NUMBER: **1932**
PRICE: **unknown**
SIZE: **8in (20.3cm) x 9-1/2in (5cm) x 1-1/4in (3.2cm) T**

KNOWN CONTENTS:
- blue plastic comb
- blue plastic brush
- blue plastic mirror with image of little girl

Notes:
A set with child-sized play pieces instead of doll-sized, a trend in late 1960's sets.

MERRY MANICURE

YEAR: **1968**
STOCK NUMBER: **1307**
PRICE: **unknown**
SIZE: **6in (15.2cm) x 9in (22.9cm)**

KNOWN CONTENTS:

- real emery board
- yellow plastic "Merry Manicure Case"
- cardboard box of *Kleenex* tissues
- wooden cuticle stick with paper label; "real Orange Stick"
- red plastic nail polish brush
- bottle of red *Merry* nail polish
- bottle of *Merry* nail polish remover
- bottle of pink *Merry* nail polish

Notes:
This set is very similar to the 1966 version except for the addition of play nail polish remover and the color of the manicure case.

STARS AND STRIPES NOVELTY DINNER SET

YEAR: **1969**
STOCK NUMBER:**2149**
PRICE: **unknown**
SIZE: **6-1/2in (16.5cm) x 10in (25.4cm)**

KNOWN CONTENTS:

- 2 paper napkins with red/white/blue paper rings
- 2 blue plastic plates with red/white/blue stars & stripes pattern sticker
- 2 clear plastic stem-type drinking glasses
- 2 red/white/blue paper place mats
- 2 white plastic flatware sets of spoon, fork and knife on plastic sprue

Notes:
Although copyrighted in 1969 and pictured in the 1972 catalog, this set almost certainly has the "Bicentennial" theme, the product fad that occupied most of the mid-1970's.

JEWEL BOX

YEAR: **1970**
STOCK NUMBER: **1601**
PRICE: **unknown**
SIZE: **6-1/2in (16.5cm) x 9-1/2in (5cm)**

KNOWN CONTENTS:
- green plastic beveled-edge jewel box with clear plastic lid
- pink plastic necklace
- pink plastic bracelet
- pink plastic tube of lipstick
- gold metal ring with red stone

Notes:
None

BEAUTY LITE COMPACT
with shoulder bag carrying case

YEAR: **1971**
STOCK NUMBER: **7356**
PRICE: **unknown**
SIZE: **10-1/2in (26.7cm) x 13in (7.6cm) x
        1-1/2in (3.8cm)**

KNOWN CONTENTS:
- pink plastic comb
- pink/clear plastic lipstick tube
- round pink compact
- pink plastic hairbrush
- yellow vinyl shoulder bag carrying case
- yellow plastic compartment-separated compact
  with battery-operated light (lights up
  automatically when opened-bulb included).

Notes:

This set is the largest in size package of any *My Merry* set located to date. The markings on the side give no indication as to the date, although the stock number of this set is very close to that of the Play Doctor and Play Nurse. The identification states:

**MERRY MANUFACTURING
A SUBSIDIARY OF LEISURE DYNAMICS, INC.
MINNEAPOLIS, MN 55435
Carrying case made in Hong Kong.**

The back of this box illustrates 14 *Miss Merry* products. "Miss Merry has everything…for little girls. "Safe and harmless cosmetics. Jewelry, Purses and Playsets, elegantly styled to make more real the grown up dreams of little girls".

The products shown are: Teeter Totter Watch (two styles), Flight Bag, Visiting Nurse, Beauty Light, Beauty Lite Compact (this set), Turtle Jewel Box, Owl Jewel Box, Fish Jewel Box, Hot Pants Knap Sack, Mail Box Knap Sack, Purse-Ables, Rainbow Vanity Set, Shooting Star Vanity Set and make Up Kit.

BUZZ-O-MATIC 'LECTRIC SHAVER

YEAR: **1971**
STOCK NUMBER: **7320**
PRICE: **unknown**
SIZE: **5-3/4in (14.6cm) x 9in (22.9cm)**

KNOWN CONTENTS:

- red plastic electric shaver with yellow label
- genuine AA battery with *Miss Merry* markings
- yellow plastic play charger
- yellow plastic cord with red plastic plugs

Notes:

An interesting toy because it actually came with a battery, something almost unheard of in the 1960's and 1970's.

MANICURE

YEAR **1971**
STOCK NUMBER: **7307**
PRICE: **unknown**
SIZE: **6-1/2in (16.5cm) x 9-1/2in (5cm) x
1in (2.5cm)**

KNOWN CONTENTS:
- green plastic *Merry* tissue box cover
- cardboard box of *Kleenex* tissues
- blue plastic nail polish brush
- glass bottle containing pink *Merry* nail polish
- glass bottle containing yellow/clear
  Merry play remover
- glass bottle containing dark pink *Merry* nail polish

Notes:
The identification on this box states:
**MERRY MANUFACTURING
A SUBSIDIARY OF LEISURE DYNAMICS, INC.
MINNEAPOLIS, MN 55435**
Carrying case made in Hong Kong.
There is nothing printed on the back of the blister card.

YEAR: 1971
STOCK NUMBER: 7305
PRICE: unknown
SIZE: 6-1/2in (16.5cm) x 9-1/2in (5cm) x
   1 in (2.5cm)

KNOWN CONTENTS:
- cardboard box of *Kleenex* tissues
- green plastic *Merry* tissue box cover
- pink plastic holder for *Merry* powder
- pink powder puff
- pink cake of *Merry* play powder
- three green plastic make-up sticks, 2 red and one
  blue

Notes:
The identification on this box states:
   MERRY MANUFACTURING
   A SUBSIDIARY OF LEISURE DYNAMICS, INC.
   MINNEAPOLIS, MN 55435
   Carrying case made in Hong Kong.
There is nothing printed on the back of the blister card.

PLAY DOCTOR KIT

YEAR **1971**
STOCK NUMBER: **7336**
PRICE: **unknown**
SIZE: **12in (5cm) x 10in (25.4cm)**

KNOWN CONTENTS:
- black plastic doctor's satchel with "Doctor Kit" sticker
- blue plastic stethoscope
- red hypodermic syringe
- yellow wooden pencil
- cardboard box of *Merry* cotton
- clear plastic bottle of colored gumballs
- cardboard *Merry* prescription pad

Notes:

This set, #7336, is almost an exact match to #1336. The stethoscope is all blue, the hypodermic needle red instead of white and then pills have been replaced with gumballs. By far, the most unique aspect of this set is the printing on the cardboard handle:

**MERRY MANUFACTURING
MINNEAPOLIS, MN 55435
A SUBSIDIARY OF LEISURE DYNAMICS, INC.
© MERRY MFG. CO. 1971**

This is the first time that the author has encountered any reference to Leisure Dynamics and is no doubt, one of the last companies to either own or license the Merry name.

YEAR **1971**
STOCK NUMBER: 7337
PRICE: **unknown**
SIZE: **12in (5cm) x 10in (25.4cm)**

KNOWN CONTENTS:
- white plastic nurse satchel with "Nurse Kit" sticker
- white cardboard nurse's cap w/elastic band
- silver plastic blunt-edged scissors
- cardboard box of *Curad* bandages
- small white paper roll of *Merry* bandages
- cardboard box of *Merry* steri-aids
- clear plastic bottle of tiny gumballs
- clear plastic thermometer

Notes:
One has to surmise that this set, #7337, would be almost an exact match to #1337, if #1337 exists. The same marking on the handle is present:
MERRY MANUFACTURING
MINNEAPOLIS, MN 55435
A SUBSIDIARY OF LEISURE DYNAMICS, INC.
© MERRY MFG. CO. 1971

ACTION SHAVER

YEAR: **unknown**
STOCK NUMBER: **7861**
PRICE: **unknown**
SIZE: **8-1/2in (21.6cm) x 12-1/2in (5cm)**

KNOWN CONTENTS:
- black plastic power cord with red plugs
- yellow plastic shaver with sticker
- yellow plastic power pack with sticker

Notes:
The only identifying information is:
MERRY MANUFACTURING
A SUBSIDIARY OF LEISURE DYNAMICS, INC.
MINNEAPOLIS, MN 55435
Made in Hong Kong.

JUNIOR MEDIC

YEAR: **unknown**
STOCK NUMBER: **7441**
PRICE: **unknown**
SIZE: **7in (17.8cm) x 10in (25.4cm)**

KNOWN CONTENTS:

- red plastic reflex hammer
- blue plastic eye glasses
- blue plastic ear scope
- clear plastic thermometer
- silver plastic head band reflector
- blue medical sponge with paper sleeve
- red plastic tongue depressor

Notes:
The only identifying information is:
MERRY MANUFACTURING
A SUBSIDIARY OF LEISURE DYNAMICS, INC.
MINNEAPOLIS, MN 55435
Made in Hong Kong.

PATIO
BARBECUE

YEAR: **unknown**
STOCK NUMBER: **7802**
PRICE: **unknown**
SIZE: **7in (17.8cm) x 10H**

KNOWN CONTENTS:
- green plastic tongs
- cardboard box of *Merry* charcoal
- orange plastic grill with stick-on picture
- 3 red plastic wieners
- black plastic cooking fork
- red/white checkered napkins

Notes:
The only identifying information is:
   MERRY MANUFACTURING
   A SUBSIDIARY OF LEISURE DYNAMICS, INC.
   MINNEAPOLIS, MN 55435
   Made in Hong Kong.

Arco Merry Toys

As with the blister-carded era chapter, this is only a representative of what was produced by Arco Toys, a Mattel licensee/subsidiary. Truly the Arco Merry toys represent the end of an era in post-war toys. Who knows, maybe the Merry name will be resurrected by the toy giant someday!

YEAR: **1978**
STOCK NUMBER: **7617**
PRICE: **unknown**
SIZE: **8-1/2in (21.6cm) x 12-1/2in (5cm)**

KNOWN CONTENTS:
- red plastic CB radio microphone
- black plastic power cord with red plugs
- red plastic CB radio with sticker

Notes:
Truly a toy representative of the era!

DATE: **1979**
STOCK NUMBER: **7702**
PRICE: **unknown**
SIZE: **8in (20.3cm) x 11in (2.5cm) x 2-1/2in (5cm)**

KNOWN CONTENTS:
- 5 white with blue floral stickered imitation *Corningware* plates and pots
- blue plastic play thermometer
- blue plastic handle
- brown and beige plastic friction-powered microwave oven

Notes:

This set has the same date, box size and stock number as a blender set. The box also states "Microwave oven really work!" This is obviously, a very poor English translation from the manufacturing country of origin. Shown here, this set represents several produced in the same motif and even in the same size package. Some others in this series include a blender, popcorn maker and hand mixer. These sets look less like the early Merry toys and more like the generic "play house" type of toys still available at toy stores today.

VISITING NURSE

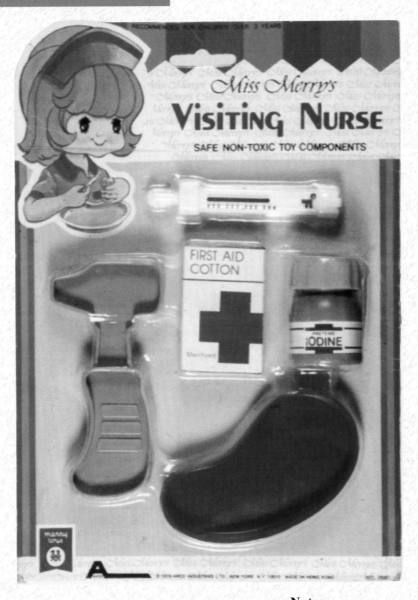

DATE: **1979**
STOCK NUMBER: **7640**
PRICE: **unknown**
SIZE: **7-1/4in (10.2cm) x 10-1/4in (10.2cm) x 1-1/2in (3.8cm)**

KNOWN CONTENTS:

- white plastic syringe
- blue plastic reflex hammer
- cardboard box of first aid cotton
- blue plastic iodine bottle with yellow cap
- kidney-shaped red plastic bowl

Notes:
The absence of any name-brand products in this set seems to be indicative of the trend that Merry products had been practicing for some time.

DATE: **1981**
STOCK NUMBER: **7507**
PRICE: **unknown**
SIZE: **8in (20.3cm) x 11in (2.5cm) x 1-1/2in (3.8cm)**

KNOWN CONTENTS:
- 10 plastic cans of *SW* brand apple juice
- 10 plastic cans of *SW* brand pineapple juice

Notes:
Cans. That's all.

PICK 'N PLAY
"Working Register, 36 Pieces"

DATE: **1981**
STOCK NUMBER: **7502**
PRICE: **unknown**
SIZE: **15in (12.7cm) x 11in (2.5cm) x 3in (7.6cm)**

KNOWN CONTENTS:

- 6 plastic trays of fixed plastic fruit
- plastic box of *Mary Lou Chocolate Cake*
- plastic box of *Ronzoni* lasagna
- plastic box of *Ronzoni* fettuccine alfredo
- 2 plastic grocery bags with "brown bag" labels
- 5 small plastic cans of *SW* and *Hunts* product
- 2 plastic boxes of *Mary Lou Cheesy Cheese Cake*
- 2 2-liter bottles of *Pepsi*
- 2 cardboard boxes of *Kellogg's Cocoa Krispies*
- 2 cardboard boxes of *Kellogg's Shredded Wheat*
- 2 cardboard boxes of *Ritz* crackers
- 2 cardboard boxes of *Kellogg's Frosted Flakes*
- beige plastic store shelf
- plastic carton of milk
- orange and yellow plastic cash register
- red and yellow plastic shopping cart
- 2 large plastic cans of *SW* brand apple juice
- 2 large plastic cans of *SW* brand pineapple juice
- 1 yellow plastic bunch of bananas

Notes:

Without a doubt, the largest "Merry" item that the author has located to date. This set has disclaimers on the package that *Pepsi*, *Nabisco* and *Fritos* are registered trademarks of their respective companies, something that earlier sets are missing. While this set lacks some of the charm of the "store" and "closet" series of the 1960's, Merry Toys was on the right track with this supermarket set. The *SW* brand must be a regional issue.

My Merry Checklist and Price Guide

Set Description	Year	Stock #	VALUES Low	High	X
The Early Period (pre 1957)					
My Merry Sets/Toys					
Beauty Shop	1952	—	$35	$65	
Boy's First Aid	1956	336	$40	$50	
Dolly's Bath Set	1955	—	$55	$75	
Dolly's Facial Kit	1953	—	$35	$40	
Dolly's First Aid	1956	—	$35	$50	
Finger and Toe Manicure	1955	—	$30	$55	
Grow-a-Garden	1953	—	$105	$220	
Manicure	1953	—	$45	$60	
Manicure	1955	11	$40	$60	
My Dolly's Merry Make-Up	1950	—	$45	$75	
Rise 'n Shine	1955	—	$50	$65	
Shampoo Set	1955	—	$55	$75	
Shaving Set	1953	—	$40	$65	
Shaving Set	1955	55	$25	$45	
Shoe Shining Set	1953	—	$65	$110	
Sonny's Shave & Shine Set	1952	—	$30	$45	
Wash-n-Wave Set (blue or white)	1950	—	$30	$45	
Wash-n-Wave Set	1953	—	$25	$45	
The Late 1950's (1957-1959 catalog)					
Beauty Shop	1957	—	$45	$60	
Beauty Shop	1959	231	$95	$125	
Bubble Horn	1959	900	$25	$45	
Dolly's Facial Kit	1957	88	$35	$60	
Dolly's First Aid	1957	521	$85	$115	
Dolly's Nail Set	1958	896	$55	$100	
Electric Shave	1957	711	$30	$45	
Make-Up	1957	33	$30	$40	
Rise 'n Shine	1957	415	$35	$65	
Shampoo Set	1957	22	$60	$65	
Shaving Set	1957	55 or 1055	$35	$45	
My Merry Closets					
Cleaning Closet	1957	C-2	$30	$40	
Dolly's Bath Closet	1958	C-9	$45	$60	
Dolly's Diaper Closet	1957	C-1	$25	$40	
Dolly's Guest Closet	1958	C-6	$27	$45	

Set Description	Year	Stock #	VALUES Low	High	X
Dolly's Hostess Closet	1958	C-8	$75	$125	
Dolly's Laundry Closet	1957	C-4	$35	$65	
Dolly's Linen Closet	1957	C-3	$30	$45	
Dolly's Over-Night Closet	1958	C-7	$30	$65	
Dolly's Party Closet	1958	C-5	$35	$75	
My Merry Stores					
Bank	1959	ST 1	$125	$125	
Drugs	1959	ST 7	$60	$100	
Hardware Store	1959	ST 5	$40	$85	
Ice Cream Shop	1959	ST 3	$35	$80	
Infant's Shop	1959	ST 2	$35	$90	
Stationery Store	1959	ST 4	$45	$95	
Supermarket	1959	ST 6	$55	$125	
My Merry Rack Sets					
Cleaning Set	1959	RC2L	$25	$80	
Coloring Set	1959	R595L	$25	$75	
Dolly's Diaper Set	1959	RC1L	$25	$75	
Dolly's Gift Wrap Set	1959	R591L	$25	$80	
Dolly's Party Set	1959	RC5L	$25	$80	
Electric Shave	1959	R597L	$25	$55	
Make-Up	1959	R33L	$25	$75	
Manicure	1959	R11L	$25	$75	
Shampoo Set	1959	R22L	$25	$75	
Shaving Set	1959	R55L	$25	$45	
Early 1960's (1961 catalog-based)					
My Merry Sets/Toys					
Beauty Shop	1960	1231	$95	$125	
Bubble Horn	1959	1900	$25	$45	
Dolly's Facial Kit	1960	1088 or 88	$30	$40	
Dolly's First Aid	1960	1521	$85	$115	
Electric Shave	1960	1711	$55	$85	
Make-Up	1960	1033	$35	$45	
Manicure	1960	1011	$35	$45	
Rise 'n Shine	1960	1415	$55	$75	
Shampoo Set	1960	1022	$30	$40	
Shaving Set	1957	1055	$35	$45	
My Merry Closets					
Cleaning Closet	1960	2002 or C-2	$35	$60	
Dolly's Diaper Closet	1960	2001 or C-1	$25	$40	
Dolly's Hostess Closet	1960	2008 or C8	$150	$225	
Dolly's Kitchen Closet	1960	2010 or C10	$65	$175	
Dolly's Linen Closet	1960	2003 or C-3	$30	$55	
Dolly's Party Closet	1960	2005 or C-5	$65	$85	
Toy Closet	1960	2011 or C11	$65	$150	

Set Description	Year	Stock #	VALUES		X
			Low	High	
My Merry Stores					
Cosmetic Shop	1960	3011	$45	$70	
Drugs	1959	3007	$60	$70	
Hardware Store	1959	3005	$0	$35	
Hobby Shop	1960	3008	$35	$45	
Ice Cream Shop	1959	3003	$0	$35	
Infant's Shop	1959	3002		$50	
Jewelry Shop	1960	3010	$175	$180	
Service Station	1960	3009	$90	$200	
Stationery Store	1959	3004	$45	$55	
Supermarket	1959	3006	$0	$45	
My Merry Rack Sets					
Coloring Set	1961	4595	$30	$65	
Dolly's Gift Wrap Set	1961	4591 or R591L	$30	$65	
Dolly's Beauty Parlor	1961	4774	$30	$75	
Dolly's Outdoor Set	1961	4775	$30	$70	
Dolly's Tea Party	1961	4772	$30	$75	
Electric Shave	1961	4597	$30	$65	
Gas Station Set	1961	4603	$30	$100	
Jewelry Set	1961	4604	$30	$75	
Make Up	1961	4033	$30	$65	
Nail Polish Set	1961	4011	$30	$75	
Nurses' Set	1961	4773	$30	$85	
Picnic Set	1961	4771	$30	$75	
Shampoo Set	1961	4022 or R22L	$30	$70	
Shaving Set	1961	4055	$30	$70	
Tea Set	1961	4602 or R602L	$30	$75	
My Merry Magic					
Bewitched Ring	1961	5105	$5	$25	
Counter Merchandiser Assortment	1961	5035	—	—	
Elusive Pegs	1961	5111	$5	$25	
Enchanted Bottle	1961	5106	$5	$25	
Haunted Cabinet	1961	5108	$5	$25	
Magic Cash Register	1961	5109	$5	$25	
Magic Rack Assortment	1961	5472	—	—	
Mystery Bolt	1961	5112	$5	$25	
Mystic Colors	1961	5104	$5	$25	
Phantom Coin	1961	5110	$5	$25	
Secret Sword	1961	5107	$5	$25	
Spirit Card Box	1961	5101	$5	$25	
Voodoo Cups	1961	5102	$5	$25	
Wizard's Dice	1961	5103	$5	$25	
Miss Merry Sets	1961				
Miss Merry at a Bar-B-Que	1961	6261	$25	$45	
Miss Merry Gives a Tea Party	1961	6263	$75	$75	

Set Description	Year	Stock #	Low	High	X
			VALUES		

Set Description	Year	Stock #	Low	High	X
Miss Merry Has a Picnic	1961	6265	$25	$45	
Miss Merry Plays Outside	1961	6264	$25	$45	
Miss Merry Plays School	1961	6262	$25	$45	
Early-mid 1960's (1963 catalog through 1966)					
Miss Merry Sets/Toys (miss or mister merry's)					
Beauty Bath	1963	1109	$25	$60	
Beauty Sleep	1963	1107	$25	$60	
Glamour Nails	1963	1108	$35	$60	
Hospital Set	1963	1115	$35	$65	
Lectric Shave	1963	1121	$25	$55	
Model's Make-Up	1963	1105	$25	$55	
Party Glamour	1963	1111	$30	$60	
Play Lighter Set	1963	1110	$25	$55	
Powder 'n Perfume	1963	1114	$25	$55	
Pretty Face	1963	1103	$25	$50	
Pretty Hair	1963	1102	$25	$55	
Pretty Lips 'n Fingertips	1963	1113	$30	$60	
Pretty Nails	1963	1101	$25	$55	
Really Neat	1963	1120	$35	$70	
Slick Shave	1963	1104 or 4104	$25	$55	
Visiting Nurse	1963	1106	$30	$65	
Miss Merry Rack Sets(miss or mister merry's)					
Baby Merry	1964	4350	$25	$45	
Beauty Bath	1963	4209	$35	$55	
Beauty Sleep	1963	4207	$35	$55	
Brush-On Beauty	1966	1323	$10	$20	
Donna Reed paper doll	1964	6403	$75	$155	
Glamour Nails	1963	4208	$35	$55	
Hospital Set	1963	4115	$35	$55	
Jo paper doll	1964	6502	$75	$130	
Jodi paper doll	1964	4362	$75	$75	
Jodi Purse Doll in yellow "Go-Go Time" case	1966	1703	$20	$115	
Judy Purse Doll in yellow " Go-Go Time " case	1966	1703	$20	$115	
Lisa paper doll	1964	4352	$35	$45	
Mindy paper doll	1964	4351	$35	$45	
Model's Make-Up	1963	4205	$35	$55	
Overnighter Travel Case, blue	1967	—	$85	$110	
Party Glamour	1963	4111	$35	$55	
Play Lighter Set	1963	4210	$35	$55	
Powder 'n Perfume	1963	4114	$35	$55	
Pretty Face	1963	4203	$35	$55	
Pretty Lips 'n Fingertips	1963	4113	$35	$55	
Pretty Nails	1963	4201	$35	$55	
Prety Hair	1963	4202	$35	$55	

Set Description	Year	Stock #	VALUES Low	High	X
Slick Shave	1963	4204	$35	$55	
Visiting Nurse	1963	4206	$35	$55	
Miss Merry Playthings					
Playthings for your Dolly's Bathroom	1963	3302	$45	$75	
Playthings for your Dolly's Den	1963	3306	$45	$65	
Playthings for your Dolly's Dining Room	1963	3305	$45	$65	
Playthings for your Dolly's Dressing Room	1963	3307	$45	$80	
Playthings for your Dolly's Kitchen	1963	3303	$45	$80	
Playthings for your Dolly's Nursery	1963	3301	$45	$120	
Playthings for your Dolly's Pantry	1963	3308	$45	$70	
Playthings for your Dolly's Party Room	1963	3304	$45	$70	
Miss Merry Barbie® Toys					
Barbie® Glamour Cosmetics	1963	1127	$300	$650	
Barbie® Makes Up	1963	1126	$150	$300	
Barbie® Manicures	1963	1125	$150	$300	
Barbie® Purse Cosmetics	1963	1123	$150	$400	
Barbie® Rouge and Powders	1963	1124	$150	$400	
Skipper®'s Bath Closet	1964	2003	$175	$275	
Skipper®'s Party Closet	1964	2001	$150	$225	
Skipper®'s Linen Closet	1964	2002	$200	$275	
Miss Merry Barbie® Rack Toys					
Barbie® Purse Cosmetics	1963	4223	$125	$250	
Barbie® Rouge and Powders	1963	4224	$125	$250	
Miscellaneous 1960's items					
"Birthday Wishes are in the Air"	—	50B-2202	$55	$145	
"Happy Birthday Little Shaver"	—	50B-2201	$55	$145	
"HAPPY BIRTHDAY"	—	50B-2205	$55	$145	
"Hope You Get Well Mighty Quick"	—	50C-2302	$55	$145	
"Hot Dawg it's your Birthday"	—	50B-2204	$55	$145	
"Perk up, Boy"	—	50C-2304	$55	$145	
"Sorry You're Sick"	—	50C-2301	$55	$145	
"To a Jewel of a Little Girl"	—	50B-2203	$55	$145	
"You Sick? Awwww!"	—	50C-2303	$55	$145	
Miss Merry Belle Doll	—	7710	$15	$25	
Miss Merry's Rainy Day Musical Jewelry Box	—	—	$55	$65	
Late 1960's (1967 catalog-based)					
Miss Merry Sets/Toys (miss or mister merry's)					
Comb 'n Curl	1967	1308	$10	$25	
Fancy Face	1967	1303	$10	$25	
Fancy Fingers	1967	1301	$10	$25	
Heavenly Hair	1967	1302	$10	$25	
Lather 'n Lotion	1967	1304	$10	$25	
Merry Manicure	1967	1307	$10	$25	
Miss Merry's Bath Time	1967	1310	$10	$25	

Set Description	Year	Stock #	VALUES		X
			Low	High	
Model's Make-Up	1967	1305	$10	$25	
Play Lighter	1967	1309	$10	$25	
Stars and Stripes Novelty Dinner Set	1967	2149	—	—	
Toy First Aid	1967	1306	$10	$35	
Toy Flash Camera	1967	1311	$10	$25	
Deluxe Sets/Toys					
Deluxe Electric Shaver Set	1967	1342	$10	$20	
Merry Beauty Bath Set	1967	1343	$10	$20	
Miss Merry's Mirror Make-Up	1967	1341	$10	$20	
Miss Merry's Overnighter	1967	1340	$10	$20	
$1 Sets/Toys					
Miss Merry's Beauty Bath	1967	1333	$20	$35	
Miss Merry's Lips, Tips 'n Hair	1967	1331	$20	$35	
Miss Merry's Make-Up	1967	1332	$20	$35	
Rise 'n Shine	1967	1335	$20	$35	
Doctor, Nurse Sets					
Play Doctor Kit	1967	1336	$20	$35	
Play Nurse Kit	1967	1337	$20	$45	
Miss Merry "Play Dress Up Jewelry"					
Counter Merchandiser Assortment	1967	1666	—	—	
Jewel Box	1967	1601	$5	$20	
Deluxe Fancy Jewelry Set	1967	1612	$5	$20	
Dress-up Diamonds	1967	1630	$5	$20	
Dress-up Pearls	1967	1631	$5	$20	
Fancy Jewelry Set	1967	1603	$5	$20	
Fancy Play Charms	1967	1613	$5	$20	
Fashion Model	1967	1633	$5	$20	
Island Princess	1967	1632	$5	$20	
Jewelry Assortment	1967	1639	—	—	
Jewelry Assortment	1967	1659	—	—	
Jewelry Assortment	1967	9166	—	—	
Jewelry Set Assortment	1967	1600	—	—	
Little Fashion Queen	1967	1932	—	—	
Mod Fashions	1967	1614	$5	$20	
Party Pearl Jewelry Set	1967	1611	$5	$20	
Petite Jewelry Set	1967	1610	$5	$20	
Play Precious Gems	1967	1602	$5	$20	
Miniature Dolls					
Bed Time Purse Doll	1967	1804	$25	$65	
Go-Go Time Purse Doll	1967	1803	$25	$65	
Party Time Purse Doll	1967	1801	$25	$65	
School Time Purse Doll	1967	1802	$25	$65	
Little Homemaker Sets					
Assortment	1967	9192	—	—	
Assortment	1967	9193	—	—	

Set Description	Year	Stock #	VALUES Low	VALUES High	X
Boy's Little Homemaker Asst.	1967	1439	—	—	
Doctor and Nurse Set Assortment	1967	1367	—	—	
Dollar Play Assortment	1967	1300	—	—	
Dolly Beauty Set Assortment	1967	1559	—	—	
Dolly Hair Styling	1967	1513	$15	$25	
Dolly Hair Tint	1967	1511	$15	$25	
Dolly Make-Up 'n Hair Tint	1967	1530	$25	$55	
Dolly Make-Up	1967	1510	$15	$25	
Dolly Shampoo 'n Rinse	1967	1512	$15	$25	
Dolly's Shampoo 'n Wave Set	1967	1531	$25	$55	
Fancy Dinner Set	1969	2112	$30	$35	
Fashion Model	1968	1658	$18	$22	
Girl's Little Homemaker Asst.	1967	1459	—	—	
Let's Be a Carpenter	1967	1436	$15	$20	
Let's Be a Repairman	1967	1437	$15	$20	
Let's Clean House	1967	1411	$25	$45	
Let's Feed Baby	1967	1412	$25	$30	
Let's Iron Clothes	1967	1413	$25	$40	
Let's Keep House	1967	1430	$25	$55	
Let's Wash 'n Iron	1967	1431	$25	$55	
Let's Wash Dishes	1967	1410	$25	$45	
Play .39 Starter Assortment	1967	1339	—	—	
Play .59 Starter Assortment	1967	1359	—	—	
Play 'Lectric Shaver	1967	1320	$25	$35	
Play Repairman	1970	1402	$10	$15	
Play Set Counter Merchandiser	1967	1366	—	—	
Early 1970's (1972 catalog-based)					
Prices are per unit, even if sold only in assortment					
Botique Play Sets	1972	7655	$15	$25	
Bracelet Bags Assortment (price per item)	1972	7020	$10	$20	
Buckle-Ups Assortment (price per item)	1972	7400	$10	$20	
Buzz-O-Matic 'Lectric Shaver	1972	7320	$10	$20	
Collars 'n Cuffs Assortment (price per item)	1972	7660	$10	$20	
Cosmetic Carry All	1972	7310	$10	$20	
Deluxe Play Set Assortment (price per item)	1972	7355	$15	$25	
Deluxe Vanity Make Up Assortment (price per item)	1972	7955	$10	$20	
Doctor 'n Nurse Kit	1972	7334	$10	$20	
Dresser Set Assortment (price per item)	1972	7900	$15	$25	
Dresser Set Assortment (price per item)	1972	7969	$10	$20	
Dress-Up Jewelry Assortment (price per item)	1972	7600	$10	$20	
Fancy Face	1972	7303	$10	$20	
Fancy Fingers	1972	7301	$10	$20	
Fancy Fragrance	1972	7308	$10	$20	
Fancy Tea and Dinner Set Assortment	1972	7169	$10	$20	
Flip Out Fun Glasses Assortment (price per item)	1972	7370	$10	$20	

Set Description	Year	Stock #	VALUES		X
			Low	High	
Jewel Box Assortment (price per item)	1972	7659	$10	$20	
Knap Sack Assortment (price per item)	1972	7070	$10	$20	
Lips, Tips 'n Curls	1972	7331	$10	$20	
Merry Make Up	1972	7332	$10	$20	
Merry Manicure	1972	7307	$10	$20	
Mickey Mouse Toy Watch	1972	7315	$10	$20	
Mirror-Comb Set Assortment (price per item)	1972	7929	$10	$20	
Model's Make-Up	1972	7305	$10	$20	
Mug Tree Assortment (price per item)	1972	7170	$10	$20	
Novelty Dinner Set and Party Assortment (sets #2149)	1972	7149	$10	$20	
Petite Perfume	1972	7314	$10	$20	
Play Doctor Kit	1972	7336	$20	$35	
Play Nurse Kit	1972	7337	$20	$45	
Purse-Ables Assortment (price per item)	1972	7042	$10	$20	
Rise 'n Shine	1972	7309	$10	$20	
Swivel Mirror and Comb Set	1972	7959	$5	$10	
Swivel Mirror Dresser Set Assortment (price per item)	1972	7901	$10	$20	
Tea and Dinner Set Assortment (price per item)	1972	7100	$10	$20	
Teeter Totter Watch	1972	7500	$10	$35	
The Birds Assortment (price per item)	1972	7700	$10	$20	
Totem Bag Assortment (price per item)	1972	7000	$10	$20	
Toy First Aid	1972	7306	$10	$20	
Toy First Aid	1972	7312	$10	$20	
Toy Flash Camera	1972	7311	$10	$20	
Vanity Tray	1972	7333	$10	$20	
Late 1970's - 1980's					
3-Room Furniture	1980	7653	$15	$30	
Action Shaver	1978	7861	$5	$15	
Afternoon Tea Service for Two	1979	7704	$20	$75	
Beauty Lite Compact	—	7356	$20	$25	
Blender	1979	7702	$15	$55	
Breakfast Time	1978	7615	$10	$15	
CB Radio	1978	7617	$10	$15	
Emergency First Aid	1978	7600	$10	$15	
Fruit Juices	1981	7507	$10	$15	
Good Morning Breakfast Set	1979	7703	$20	$75	
Hand Mixer	1979	7702	$15	$30	
Junior Medic	1978	7441	$5	$15	
Microwave Oven	1979	7702	$15	$30	
Patio Barbecue	1978	7802	$5	$15	
Pick 'n Play	1981	7502	$15	$25	
Popcorn Maker	1979	7702	$15	$30	
Shop 'n Play	1981	7502	$25	$30	
Tea Set	1979	7700	$10	$35	
Visiting Nurse	1979	7640	$15	$20	

Index

About the Author

The author, Fred Diehl, has been a toy collector for over 30 years. It started with collecting Matchbox models with his father at train shows and progressed to other toys of the 1950's and 1960's. Vintage *Never Removed From Box* (NRFB) *Barbie*® dolls and outfits are another favorite and it was this foray into "dolls" that a fascination and love of *My Merry* began. The author has written a book and magazine articles on Matchbox models for several years (store displays and gift sets are favorites) and currently writes NRFB *Barbie*® articles for *Barbie*® *Bazaar* magazine. Old cameras and automobiles are also of interest to the author. He lives in Baltimore with his son, Andy.

The author is holding a very rare *My Merry Barbie*® Manicure set, #1125 from 1963, that was acquired too late for inclusion in this book!